The
Evangelical
Essential

The Evangelical Essential

What Must I Do To Be Saved?

Philip Janowsky

VISION™
HOUSE
PUBLISHING, INC.
Gresham, Oregon 97230

THE EVANGELICAL ESSENTIAL
© 1994 by Philip W. Janowsky

Published by Vision House Publishing, Inc.
1217 NE Burnside, Suite 403
Gresham, Oregon 97030

Edited by Steve Halliday

Printed in the United States of America.

International Standard Book Number: 1-885305-07-9

Unless otherwise indicated, all Scripture references are from
the Holy Bible: New International Version, © 1973, 1978,
1984 by International Bible Society. Used by permission of
Zondervan Publishing House. All rights reserved. The "NIV"
and "New International Version" trademarks are registered
in the United States Patent and Trademark Office by
International Bible Society. Use of either trademark requires
the permission of International Bible Society.

Scripture references marked KJV are from the Holy Bible:
Authorized King James Version.

Scripture references marked NASB are from the New
American Standard Bible, The Lockman Foundation
© 1960, 1962, 1963, 1968, 1971, 1972, 1973, 1975, 1977.
Used by permission.

94 95 96 97 98 99 00 -- 7 6 5 4 3 2 1

Contents

Foreword

The Evangelical enterprise is in trouble! The exciting renaissance of Evangelicalism that began in the fifties is clearly coming untracked. Francis Schaeffer was one of the first voices to sound the warning. In 1984 in his book, *The Great Evangelical Disaster*, he detailed his reasons for serious concern. Chief among these concerns was a growing loss of the sense of biblical authority among Evangelicals, as well as a growing tendency among Evangelical scholars to compromise biblical teaching on (what we would call) "politically correct" issues in order to gain academic recognition and respectability.

Even before this, Carl Henry, one of Evangelicalism's most prominent and gifted spokespersons, also saw the storm warnings. Way back in 1967 he saw the same trend away from biblical authority in the Evangelical camp. He warned that if biblical authority continued to be eroded, "then the distinction between Scripture and tradition is greatly lessened." The result, he predicted, would be an emasculated movement unable to compete with a strong and authoritarian Roman Catholicism.[1] The defection of Thomas Howard and others associated with Evangelicalism to Catholicism has shown Henry to be prophetic on this point.

More recently, David Wells has weighed in with *No Place for Truth*.[2] One reviewer of the book, having admitted the truth of Dr. Wells' thesis, went on to suggest that if he was going to thus curse the darkness, he might also attempt to light one candle.

This study is an attempt, however feeble, to light one candle!

Philip W. Janowsky

Notes

1. Carl F. H. Henry, *Evangelicals at the Brink of Crisis*, 23.

2. David Wells, *No Place for Truth* (Grand Rapids: W.B. Eerdmans, 1993).

Chapter One

Evangelicalism Then and Now

On a recent CBS "This Morning" news broadcast, actress Dixie Carter was asked about her new video promoting yoga as a means of relaxation and renewal. She replied, "I'm evangelical about yoga. It's transforming!"[1]

Then not long ago I found myself in conversation with a mainline church leader. In the course of the conversation I mentioned I was an Evangelical. "I consider myself to be an 'Evangelical,' " she replied. Knowing well her theological stance, I asked her how she would define the term "Evangelical." She replied that she considered anyone who believed in God and preached from the Bible to be an "Evangelical." But she hastily added,

"I don't believe in the atonement!"

The word "Evangelical," as a theologically descriptive term, is rapidly becoming meaningless.

It has not always been so. In the Protestant Reformation it was that term which was first used to designate a specific theological stance. It was not applied unambiguously to all the streams of the Protestant Reformation. Rather, it was first applied to Martin Luther and his followers by his Catholic critics because of Luther's insistence on the primacy of the Pauline doctrine of justification solely by faith as found in Romans and Galatians. No more works of supererogation. No more need for penance. Simply trust in Christ alone, as St. Paul has written, and you will be justified. If true, indeed it was "good news"!

As such, "Evangelical" carried specific content. It raised both the question of religious authority and how one might be saved.

The term continued to live on in Lutheranism, but began to fade into minor importance as other streams in the Protestant movement grew in numbers and influence.

The term would not again become widely used to designate a specific religious movement until around the middle of the twentieth century.[2] It began to be used at this time to designate a movement that would hold much in common with Fundamentalism, but would seek to distinguish itself from Fundamentalism by a heightened emphasis on research and a more academic approach to the articulation and defense of historic Christianity. This would in turn give rise to the half-facetious definition of an Evangelical as a seminarian whose father had been a Fundamentalist minister.

The Evangelicalism of that time sought to confront modernism and "Christian" liberalism with sound academic research and apologetics. The founding of *Christianity Today* in 1956 under the editorial leadership of Carl F. H. Henry gave the movement a forum for the best minds in Christian orthodoxy to cross swords with the scholars of liberalism who had been having their way in academia virtually by default. C. S. Lewis, Francis Schaeffer, and Carl F. H. Henry were some of the earliest and ablest writers to come to the arena.

Meanwhile, the Billy Graham Crusades got into full swing. Departing from the earlier absolute separatist attitude of Fundamentalism, they sought to incorporate all spectra of the Christian community into cooperative evangelistic efforts. Thus the historic gospel of redemption and reconciliation through Christ's cross was preached to audiences that had not been in touch with the historic Evangelical gospel message.

The two-pronged attack thus generated began to achieve dramatic results. Mainline churches began declining in membership and attendance. Conservative churches, meanwhile, were growing. These were heady days for Fundamentalists and Evangelicals alike. The adversary was "Christian" liberalism. Christian conservatives were by and large united and focused. And they were winning!

Students who had come from Fundamentalist and Evangelical backgrounds, feeling that they now might be able to hold their own in the theological and religious debates of greater academia, began to look to the mainline seminaries and the more prestigious universities as places to do their graduate studies.

But just here a problem began to be encountered. Many

of these young students found the aura of power and academic acceptability intoxicating. Some encountered peer pressure in the discussions and academic intimidation from liberal faculty members. Little by little, contrary assumptions and viewpoints were absorbed by some who would eventually graduate and begin to occupy positions of leadership in the Evangelical community.

Back near the beginning of this grand new Evangelical adventure, Carl Henry had proposed a bold scheme for restoring historic Christianity to the mainline denominations. Pointing out that all seminaries and mainline churches (with the exception of the Unitarians) had originally been conservative theologically, he proposed that it was time for conservative scholars and ministers to re-infiltrate these institutions so that from inside one voice would be as a thousand, while outside a thousand voices would be as one.

The importance of the proposed strategy for this study is two fold. First, it underscores the assumption of unity within the Evangelical community, which was widely held at that time. Second, it causes one to ask the question, What was the one voice of the Evangelicals presumably saying?

The Twofold Strategy

First, all Evangelicals agreed with historic Christianity that Jesus Christ was, in the words of the Nicene Creed, very God and very man. The deity of Jesus was not in question. Second, Evangelicals held that justification is solely by faith in the finished work of Christ. And third, they considered the canonical Scriptures of the Old and New Testaments as the *final* authority on all matters of faith and practice. While tradition, reason, and experience could be consulted, Scripture is always magisterial while the others are ministerial. These beliefs were and are the bedrock of both Fundamentalism and Evangelicalism.

But then two things began to happen. First, certain "politically correct" agendas began to challenge the clear assumptions of Scripture. Probably the first of these challenges came from the feminist movement. Following close on the heels of the feminist movement came the pro-choice or abortion movement. And last, but certainly not least, came the gay rights movement.

C. S. Lewis once wrote an essay about circles and their power over people. He pointed out that once these inner circles are formed, they have a life and power of their own. It seems to those who form these circles that they are the only intelligent and informed people in the world. An elitism sets in. Gaining entrance to that circle seems so desirable to those outside looking in that they will do practically anything—including compromising their own integrity—to gain access. One of the reasons Lewis never got the recognition at Oxford that he so richly deserved was that in becoming an apologist for historic Christianity, he was scorned by some of his peers who controlled that particular circle at the University.

These "politically correct" agendas form just such circles. Defense of these issues is considered to be *prima facie* evidence to the rest within the circle of superior intelligence and academic ability. Those who hold contrary positions are dismissed as intellectual inferiors who simply "don't get it."

Thus, in efforts to appear "with it" and politically correct, *some* evangelical scholars began to subject the

Scriptures to the Procrustean bed of political correctness. The results? On the univocal teaching of Scripture against the gay lifestyle, for example, arguments such as "it didn't even make the Ten Commandments" and "Jesus never mentioned it" began to be put forth—patently specious arguments that are credible to the user only because they allow one to remain in the politically correct circle.

But a second thing also took place. While it was much more subtle, it began to acquire equal importance. A shift in biblical interpretation began to occur within the "Evangelical" camp.

Paul vs. Jesus

It has already been noted that politically correct agendas began to cause some Evangelical scholars to look for ways to re-interpret certain Scriptures that offended some. Now it must be noted that, by and large, these "offensive" Scriptures, when found in the New Testament, are located in the letters of Paul to the New Testament churches. Many feminists have taken umbrage at Paul's remarks about women and "silence" in the churches, seemingly unaware that his seating of women as equals with men in the assembly of the churches constitutes the first recorded incident of its kind in the history of civilization. Also it is Paul who refers to the homosexual practices of both men and women in the Roman empire as *prima facie* evidence that mankind is in rebellion against God (Romans 1:18-31).

The playing off of Jesus against Paul is at least as old as Albert Schweitzer. In fact, it is considerably older than that, having first occurred, according to W. H. C. Frend, late in the third century in conjunction with the rise of the monastic movement.[3] This is an extremely important point to be remembered and will be developed later in this study. At present it is enough to observe that with the rise of "politically correct" agendas, the trend to appeal to the teachings of Jesus (or lack of them on certain subjects), to the detriment of Pauline authority, has become a discernible trend in present day "Evangelicalism" (*see* chapter 8).

This trend has been accelerated by the emergence of Anabaptist theologians within the "Evangelical" ranks. While continental Anabaptism originated during the Reformation, it was not soteriologically or hermeneutically one with Luther and Calvin. Both Luther and Calvin saw Anabaptism as an enemy to what they were doing. The Evangelical Reformers used the doctrine of justification solely by faith and the writings of Paul—especially Romans—as the paradigm through which to interpret the rest of Scripture. The Anabaptists, to the contrary, used the ethical teachings of Jesus to understand the rest of Scripture. The Pauline doctrine of *sola fide* was not central to their soteriology.

One Voice to Several Voices

These, then, are some of the reasons why the "one voice" of the early days of Carl Henry's *Christianity Today* has now become several voices. The question must now be asked, Does Evangelical orthodoxy exist? And if so, which is the true Evangelical voice?

The topic of this study is *Evangelicalism and the Apostolic Tradition.* The Apostolic Tradition is, of course, the earliest observable tradition in Christianity. It has its origins in the first Jerusalem Conference (*see* Acts 15, ca. A.D. 49), where the discussion of how one is "saved" in the Christian dispensation was settled in favor of Paul. Later the creeds would articulate basic Christian theology. An alternate view to Apostolic soteriology would later develop and become known as Roman Catholicism.

It is the thesis of this study that the Apostolic Tradition is the original and purest tradition, and that Evangelicalism and the Apostolic Tradition are ONE.

Notes

1. CBS "This Morning," 11 April 1994.

2. In Third World countries such as Latin America, the term "Evangelical" has long been used to describe non-Catholic groups by Roman Catholics, who do not so easily forget church history!

3. W. H. C. Frend, *The Rise of Christianity* (Philadelphia: Fortress Press, 1984), 54.

Chapter Two

Let's Come to Terms

Before going farther, it would be well to make one thing clear. This study is not an attempt to "deChristianize" Anabaptism, Roman Catholicism, or Eastern Orthodoxy. The assumption of this study is that of St. Paul when he wrote, "That if you confess with your mouth, 'Jesus is Lord,' and believe in your heart that God raised him from the dead, you will be saved" (Romans 10:9).

It is also the assumption of this study that the Apostolic Tradition as found in the documents of the New Testament—and especially the work and writing of Paul—is the earliest and purest tradition. Since this is the tradition that was rediscovered by Luther and the Evangelical

Reformers during a dark hour in church history, the thesis that Evangelicalism and the Apostolic Tradition are ONE will now be developed.

How Old Is Evangelicalism?

There is some confusion about exactly when the modern Evangelical movement arose. Many scholars tend to place its origins in the English revivals of Wesley and Whitefield.[1] John Gerstner, former professor of church history at Pittsburgh Theological Seminary, is undoubtedly correct in identifying the origin of the use of the term "Evangelical" in its modern sense as occurring in the Protestant Reformation:

> Despite the dominant usage of *euangellismo* in the New Testament, its derivative, evangelical, was not widely or controversially employed until the Reformation period. Then it came into prominence with Martin Luther precisely because he reasserted Paul's teaching on the *Euangelismos* as the indispensable message of salvation. The essence of the saving message for Luther was justification by faith alone, the article by which not only the church stands or falls but each individual as well. Erasmus, Thomas More, and Johannes Eck denigrated those who accepted this view and referred to them as "evangelicals."[2]

There are two observations in this statement that demand particular attention. The first is that Luther was not referring to justification by faith in some nebulous way. He was "reasserting Paul's teaching" on the meaning of justification by faith. The second thing that deserves notice is that Erasmus was one of the originators of the appellation "Evangelical" as a descriptive term for Luther and his followers; it derived precisely from Luther's insistence on Paul's doctrine of justification by faith alone. Erasmus would later give aid to a lesser-known current within the Protestant Reformation called Anabaptism.[3] As this study progresses, the relevance of these points will become increasingly clear.

It may be concluded that the term "Evangelical" as it applies to a specific movement within Christianity, originated during the Protestant Reformation. It was used to describe Luther and his immediate followers. When we recall that it was in hearing Luther's preface to Romans read one fateful night at Aldersgate Street Meeting House that John Wesley received his heartwarming experience which triggered the English "Evangelical" revival, we can appreciate that "Evangelicalism" has its taproot in the beginnings of the Reformation. Thus it is to the Protestant Reformation that we now turn.

The Protestant Reformation

The story of the Protestant Reformation and the story of Martin Luther and his place in the Reformation are well known and thus do not demand complete reconstruction here. The nailing of the ninety-five theses to the door of the Wittenberg Church set the theological debate in motion, and Luther's debate with Johannes von Eck at Worms became the decisive battle.

The central question raised by the ninety-five theses was soteriological: "What must I do to be saved?" The answer that Paul gave the Phillipian jailer brought peace to Luther's tormented soul. "Believe on the Lord Jesus Christ and thou shalt be saved." The central issue raised at Worms was the question of authority—who says this is what one must do to be saved? Luther's answer: Scripture, apart from the traditions of the church. Scripture and Scripture alone. "Unless I am convinced by testimonies of Scripture and plain reason—I do not accept the authority of popes and councils, for they have contradicted each other—my conscience is captive to the word of God. I cannot and I will not recant anything, for to go against conscience is neither right nor sane, God help me. Amen."[4] Thus the principles of justification solely by faith and the sole authority of Scripture in matters of faith and practice are the twin cornerstones on which the Protestant Reformation rests.

But a question arises: What was the position of the Roman Catholic church on Scripture? Had Scripture been entirely set aside? And if not, what made Luther's interpretation of the nature of salvation so remarkable and different from that of the church in which he had been ordained?

Protestants often assume that the Catholic church of Luther's day held a low view of Scripture. Such was not the case. The Council of Trent which was called on April 18, 1546, during the height of the Reformation, published the Roman Catholic position concerning Scripture with these words:

The holy, ecumenical and general Council of Trent, lawfully assembled in the Holy Ghost, the same three legates of the Apostolic See presiding, keeps this constantly in view, namely, that the purity of the Gospel may be preserved in the Church. . . . This [Gospel], of

old promised through the prophets in the Holy
Scriptures, our Lord Jesus Christ, the Son of God, pro-
mulgated first with his own mouth, and then commanded it to be preached by His apostles to every
creature as the course at once of all saving truth and
rules of conduct. It also clearly perceives that these
truths and rules are contained in the written books
and in the unwritten traditions, which, received by
the Apostles themselves, the Holy Ghost dictating,
have come down to us, transmitted as it were from
hand to hand. Following, then, the examples of the
orthodox Fathers, it receives and venerates with a
feeling of piety and reverence all the books both of
the Old and of the New Testaments, since one God is
the author of both, and also the traditions, whether
they relate to faith or to morals, as having been dic-
tated either orally by Christ or by the Holy Ghost,
and preserved in the Catholic Church in unbroken
succession.[5]

The importance of this statement by the Catholic magisterium cannot be overemphasized. While it reveals a very
high view of biblical inspiration, it also reveals the crux of
Luther's problem. The Catholic hierarchy was willing to
give the same inspiration and authority to the extra-
biblical, ongoing traditions of the church, as it was to
Scripture itself. Indeed, it had shown itself willing to grant
greater authority to the ongoing traditions, in that though
they could not be adduced from Scripture (i.e., the sale of
indulgences for the forgiveness of sins), they were inspired
of the Holy Spirit and thus authoritative to the point of
canonicity! While not denying the possibility of ongoing
revelation by the Holy Spirit, Luther asserted that ongoing

revelation will never contradict the Scripture and must be tested by Scripture. He also asserted that ongoing revelation can never have the universal authority in the church that Scripture has.

But this was only one of Luther's difficulties with the Catholic handling of Scripture. Early on he had embarked on a career in law at the University of Erfurt. One day while doing research in the library, he came across an entire Bible. Though baptized, confirmed, and raised in the Catholic church, he had never seen an entire Bible. The homilies prepared for worship service contained only bits and pieces of Scripture. And even those were in Latin rather than in his native language. Before that day he had no idea that there was so much more to the Bible. J. H. Merle D'Aubigne describes this crucial moment:

> He has never until this hour seen its like. He reads the title; it is the Bible, a rare book, unknown in those times. His interest is greatly excited; he is filled with astonishment at finding other matters than those fragments of the gospels and epistles that the church has selected to be read to the people during public worship every Sunday throughout the year. Until this day he had imagined that they composed the whole word of God. And now he sees so many pages, so many chapters, so many books of which he had no idea. His heart beats as he holds the divinely inspired volume in his hand. With eagerness and with indescribable emotion he turns over these leaves from God . . . "O that God would give me such a book for myself," thought he.[6]

It seems clear from succeeding events that Luther did not quickly conclude from those new vistas of Scripture that the Catholic position on soteriology was incorrect. The Catholic church taught that Christ was uniquely God's Son, born of the Virgin; He had lived a sinless life, and while His death on the Cross was the means of mankind's salvation, the salvation won by Christ must be merited by the believer.

In other words, one must merit this merit of Christ. The believer must embark on a lifelong journey of confession, penance, and good works. The aim of this journey is to achieve perfection in this life. For those who do not, the terrors of purgatory wait. Those who do are declared "saints" and allowed to go directly into the presence of God at death.

Escaping purgatory through achieving sainthood was much to be desired. The trouble was that only those who left secular vocations to embark upon a life of prayer, meditation, mortification, and good works in some religious order had any chance of achieving perfection (sainthood) in this life. Jesus' words to the rich young ruler, "If thou wilt be perfect, go and sell what thou hast, and give to the poor, and thou shalt have treasure in heaven: and come and follow me" (Matthew 19:21, KJV), had been the cry of the monastic movement from its very inception.[7] This was why Luther eventually left his studies in law at Erfurt, and entered the Augustinian monastery at Wittenberg.

The Roman Catholic system of achieving justification is so foreign to contemporary Protestantism as a result of Luther's work that we often take it for granted that this, too, was the product of extra-biblical Catholic tradition and has no real root in the Scriptures. Such is not the case! Roman Catholic soteriology is based on a tradition of biblical interpretation that began late in the third century.

The Rise of the Monastic Movement

For the first three centuries, the Christian church had followed the theology and soteriology of the apostle Paul as the hermeneutical paradigm for interpreting Scripture.[8] The rise of the monastic movement would change all that. Turning away from Paul and embracing the ethical teachings of the earthly Jesus—especially the admonition to the rich young ruler (Matthew 19:21)—the monastic movement was born. No longer was salvation a matter of trust in the finished atonement and appropriating its merit by faith. Now one must achieve ethical perfection by divesting oneself of property, removing oneself from the real world with its multiplicity of temptations, and entering the artificial world of the monastery.

And what of those ordinary Christians who could not take this avenue to perfection? Paul's answer had been a simple one: justification is by faith. All of mankind may come in at this door.

Having turned away from Pauline soteriology, the Catholic church was now faced with a multiplicity of soteriological questions. Catholic casuistry was born. So steeped was the Catholic church of Luther's time in the view that salvation was achieved by tortuously following the teachings and example of the earthly Jesus, aided by the church's prescribed penances and meritorious works—rather than through simple, trusting faith in the atonement—that the place of Paul as the "chosen vessel" (Acts 9:15) to interpret Christ's mission had largely been forgotten.

Luther's search for peace with God led him to take the final step prescribed by the Catholic church for achieving perfection in this life. In leaving everything behind and in joining the Augustinian monastery at Wittenberg, he had done all that he could do to follow the teachings of Jesus. He had given up all that he had—career, possessions, and friends—according to Jesus' words to the rich young ruler, and he would now pursue only righteousness.

The peace that he received by that momentous decision was simply the calm before the real storm. For now he discovered that his proneness to failure and sin was not caused by society with its myriad temptations, but by something that was an integral part of himself. Having played the last card in the hand that had been dealt him by the church, Martin Luther was in despair.

During this time of blackness, he was drawn ever deeper into the study of the Scriptures. Now, as an ordained member of a religious order, he had the entire Bible available to him once more. The psalms and the writings of Paul especially attracted him.[9] The notes of assurance and joy fell like drops of rain into his parched soul. The seventeenth verse of Romans 1, "The just shall live by faith," gripped his mind. He fastened to it like a drowning man to a straw.

It is perhaps idle to speculate on the exact time and place where the real significance of Romans 1:17 was revealed. But what took place in Luther's mind and soul as a result is of paramount importance to our understanding of the Reformation and of the beginnings of Evangelicalism. Here are Luther's own words:

At last, God being merciful, as I meditated day and night on the connection of the words, namely, "the justice of God is revealed in it, as it is written, 'The just shall live by faith,' " there I began to understand the justice of God as that by which the just live, by the gift of God, namely by faith . . . This immediately made me feel as if I was reborn, and as though I had entered through open gates into paradise itself. From then on, the whole face of Scripture appeared different.[10]

The Reformation was under way.

The Church's Primary Theologian

We have already established that the primitive church followed the teachings of the risen Christ as given by the Holy Spirit to the apostle Paul. Paul was understood to be the theologian of primitive Christianity. His soteriology was followed for the first three centuries.[11] Even into the fourth century, the Pauline doctrine of justification solely by faith was held to be the mark of Christian orthodoxy. In responding to the Ebionite heresy that had risen within the church, Eusebius wrote, "They held that they must observe every detail of the Law—by faith in Christ alone, and a life built upon that faith, they would never win salvation." He goes on to say of the Ebionites, "They held that the epistles of the Apostle ought to be rejected altogether. . . ."[12] The apostle here referred to is Paul.

Thus we may correctly observe that one of the earliest heresies which the Christian church had to contend with, Ebionism, was based on a declension from the writings and theology of Paul. We may also correctly observe that monasticism as a movement was based on a rejection of the hermeneutical importance of the writings and theology of Paul by giving the ethical teachings of the earthly Jesus a significance which they had not previously enjoyed.[13] The monastic movement eventually gave theological and soteriological content to what would become Roman Catholicism. The Reformation represents a rediscovery and reassertion of Paul as the church's primary theologian.

Wesleyan Evangelicalism

While Evangelicalism in its modern form did not originate in the time of John and Charles Wesley, it may be said that Evangelicalism came to "full flower" under the preaching of the Wesleys and of George Whitefield. We can therefore benefit from an examination of that revival in order to determine its similarities and differences with the continental Evangelicalism which preceded it.

The story of the "conversion" of the Wesleys, like the story of Martin Luther, is quite well known. Reared in the home of an Anglican parish priest, both boys elected to follow in their father's footsteps and enter professional ministry. To that end both went to Oxford University and began a serious study of Anglican polity and theology.

Because the Anglican church was the church of the Wesleys, it is often assumed they were raised in a Protestant theological atmosphere. Such is not the case. While the Church of England had indeed broken with Rome politically in the early part of the sixteenth century, the basic elements of Roman Catholic theology were still largely intact. Catholic theology—and in particular, Catholic soteriology—were essentially the same as they had been for Luther and Zwingli prior to the Reformation.

As early as the fifteenth century, John Wycliffe, an English priest, had set in motion the translation of the

Scriptures into the vernacular. William Tyndale had carried on this work of translation during the reign of Henry VIII. Tyndale's work of translation was bitterly opposed and it resulted in his martyrdom.[14] But the results of having placed the Bible in the hands of the English laity would continue to act as a ferment until other corrections in church procedure and practice would take place.

Of great significance is the fact that while the giving of the Bible to the English people prompted such changes as the ability of the priests to marry and the receiving of the communion of both kinds (bread and wine) by the laity, the question of how one is saved remained essentially the historic position of the Roman Catholic Church. The authority of Scripture had become a principle in the Church of England, but this did not immediately lead to the cardinal doctrine of Evangelicalism, the doctrine of justification solely by faith.

"There was a basic principle in Wesley's thought at this period in his life," writes William Ragsdale Canon, "the principle that man must be saved through moral goodness, through universal obedience, and through the rigid fulfillment of all the commandments of God."[15] The moral theology of Anglicanism taught that "Christ died for all if all will take care to perform the conditions required by Him."[16] George Bull, an Anglican theologian, had written, "Justification signifies that love of God by which he embraces those who are already leading a holy life, and determines them to be worthy of the reward of life eternal through Christ."[17] Canon goes on to say of Wesley, "He had no conception whatever of the love of the Father shed abroad in the hearts of his children. He believed that the gift of Christ's atonement had to be achieved through man's own efforts, through moral goodness. . . ."[18]

Under the stress of identical soteriological assumptions, Martin Luther had fled to the monastery. If the ethical teachings of the earthly Jesus (especially the Sermon on the Mount) were to be followed as the pathway to perfection, one must give up personal possessions. One must extinguish desire for the opposite sex. Therefore Luther had renounced career, friends, possessions, and sought the cloister away from the temptations that vex humanity.

The Church of England had divested itself of monasteries or John Wesley might have accepted that avenue also. But since the cloister was closed to him and since he was under similar duress, Wesley decided to go to Georgia as a pastor to a British colony in the New World, as a missionary to the natives. That it was his fervent hope that he would achieve the ethical perfection still regarded as essential for entrance into eternal life by going to Georgia, is evident through these words written in a letter composed to explain the venture:

> Toward mortifying the desire of the flesh, the desire of the sensual pleasures, it will be no small thing to be able, without fear of giving offense, to live on water and the fruits of the earth. This simplicity of food will, I trust, be a blessed means, which God designed should be found only in faith in love and joy in the Holy Ghost; and it will assist me—especially where I see no woman but those which are almost of a different species from me—to attain such a purity of thought as suits a candidate for that state wherein they neither marry nor are given in marriage.[19]

Wesley's reference to seeing only women of an almost entirely different species (American Indian women) reflected more than just the hope that he would find Indian maidens unattractive and thus not be incited to desire. It also reflected the popular notion (which is still shared in many quarters) that society was the real reason for the sinfulness of mankind. The unspoiled and noble savage was one of the prevailing myths of that time. Wesley had not yet become seriously acquainted with Pauline anthropology. He still did not believe that the fall of Adam had infected the whole human race.

Wesley wrote to Dr. John Burton just four days before leaving for Georgia, "I hope to learn the true sense of the gospel of Christ by preaching it to the heathen. They have no comments to construe away the text; no vain philosophy to corrupt it; no luxurious, sensual, covetous, ambitious expounders to soften its unpleasing truths. . . . They are all little children, humble, willing to learn, and eager to do the will of God."[20]

Arriving in Georgia, Wesley discovered that he had left what he had thought to be the cause of his inability to become perfect, only to discover that he was confronted with the same set of struggles and temptations. He fell in love with one of the daughters of a Georgia colonist but could not bring himself to marry her.[21] His firsthand contact with the American Indians utterly shattered any lingering notions about civilization and its material temptations being the chief cause of sin.[22] He began to realize the dismal truth. His problems and the problems of the human race were not caused from without but from within. Wesley had empirically discovered the Pauline doctrine of universal human depravity.

The Methodist mission to Georgia was a fiasco. Leaving under cover of night to escape trial on civil charges, Wesley in bitterness of spirit made his way north where he boarded a ship back to England. But three things of great importance had happened. First, he had come to the point of despair of obtaining spiritual perfection through personal effort. Second, any notions he had entertained concerning the basic purity and innocence of human nature when freed from the corrupting influence of society were irreparably shattered. Third, he had made the acquaintance of some Moravian missionaries who in turn had begun to introduce him to the Pauline writings as the key to salvation.

Charles Wesley had left the Georgia mission much earlier than John. While back in England, he had become friends with the Moravian, Peter Bohler. Bohler began challenging both John and Charles to read Paul on the question of salvation by faith.

Suddenly the Wesleys began to hear Paul give theological and anthropological meaning to what they had existentially experienced. Through Adam all have sinned and fallen. We are all by nature enemies of God. We cannot help ourselves. We must cease seeking righteousness through personal endeavor, and trust in the finished work of Christ.[23]

All this came to a head for John on that fateful evening when he went to the little chapel service on Aldersgate Street. The leader was reading from Martin Luther's Preface to Romans. In Wesley's own words, "About a quarter before nine, while he was describing the change which God works in the heart through faith in Christ, I felt my heart strangely warmed. I felt I did trust in Christ, Christ alone for salvation; and an assurance was given me that He had taken away my sins, even mine, and saved me from the law of sin and death."[24]

And what were the words of Luther that Wesley heard that fateful night?

The first duty of the preacher of the gospel is to declare God's law and describe the nature of sin. . . . The preacher's message must show men their lamentable state, so as to make them humble and yearn for help.

He [Paul] says that all men are sinners, and that none are approved by God. Salvation can only come to them, unearned, by virtue of faith in Christ. Christ has earned it for us through His blood. For our sakes, He had become God's "mercy seat," and so God forgives all the sins that we have committed in the past. In this way, God shows that His own righteousness, which He confers through the medium of faith, is our only hope.[25]

Wesley's journal entry for Sunday, June 4, just a little over a week after Aldersgate read, "Sun. 4—Was indeed a feast-day. For from the time of my rising till past one in the afternoon, I was praying, reading the Scriptures, singing praise, or calling sinners to repentance. All these days I scarce remember to have opened the Testament but upon some great and precious promise (cf. 1 Pet. 1:14). And I saw more than ever that the gospel is in truth but one great promise from beginning to end."[26] At this point one cannot help but be reminded of Luther's words under almost identical circumstances: "From then on, the whole face of Scripture appeared different."

The Priority of Paul

This in turn brings us to a most important point. Both Luther and Wesley had enjoyed the Scriptures before them and had studied them at great length. *But only when they began to use the writings and theology of Paul as the hermeneutical paradigm*[27] *through which Scripture was to be interpreted, did they come to their Evangelical faith.* Holding Scripture as the final authority is not enough! *How one reads the Scriptures* is of equal consequence. Luther came to view Paul's letter to Rome as the Bible's own commentary upon itself, a paradigm by and through which to "rightly divide the word of truth."

The Pauline doctrine of the total depravity of man now became a prominent theme in Wesley's preaching. He wrote of man's condition, that in the natural and unregenerate state, mankind "has no more significant knowledge of God than the beasts of the field. Having no proper knowledge of God we have no love of him. . . . Every man born into the world is a rank idolater . . . Is man by nature filled with all manner of evil? Is he void of all good? Is he wholly fallen? Is his soul totally corrupted? . . . Allow this and you are so far a Christian. Deny it and you are but a heathen still."[29] In another place he would state that if the doctrine of original sin were to be lost, it would not be long before all other Christian doctrines were lost!

With this understanding of the awfulness of human depravity and the utter helplessness of the human race to save itself, came a new appreciation of the majesty and mystery of redemption through faith in the finished work of Christ. It was this note of certainty of his redemption that earned him the epithet "enthusiast."[29] He began to be barred from Anglican pulpits. After having been told that he might not preach at St. Anne's Cathedral any more, he wrote to Charles these revealing words:

> I have seen upon this occasion, more than ever I could have imagined, how intolerable the doctrine of faith is to the mind of man and how particularly intolerable to religious men. One may say the most unchristian things, even down to deism; the most enthusiastic things, so they proceed but upon mental raptures, light, and union; the most severe things, even the whole rigor of ascetic mortification; and all this will be forgiven. But if you speak of faith in such a manner as makes Christ a saviour to the utmost, a most universal help and refuge; in such a manner as takes away glorying, but adds happiness to wretched man; as discovers a greater pollution in the best of us than we could before acknowledge, but brings a greater deliverance from it than we could before expect—if any one offers to talk at this rate, he shall be heard with the same abhorrence as if he was going to rob mankind of their salvation, their mediator, or their hopes of forgiveness . . .[30]

Clearly, Wesley is one with Luther and the continental Reformers concerning the doctrine of the total depravity of man, justification by faith alone, and the authority of Scripture, understood through the writings of Paul.

He would differ from the Reformers on one important point: the question of free will. Against the determinism of the continental Reformers, Wesley would adduce biblical evidence that though man was totally fallen spiritually, man could choose to helplessly cling to the finished work of Christ for salvation, or could choose to go onward to destruction.

From Aldersgate onward, Wesley was first and foremost an evangelist. His ministry was characterized by proclamation. Hildebrandt observes, "The Word for Wesley, as for Luther, is the beginning and the end, the 'author of faith' and its final rest; for our hope is stayed on this 'faithfulness' which 'each moment we find,' and He is 'the God who always bears in mind His everlasting word.' Justification by faith is the content of Scripture and Scripture is the proof of the doctrine."[32]

Notes

1. John Warwick Montgomery, ed., *God's Inerrant Word* (Minneapolis: Bethany Fellowship, Inc., 1974), 20.

2. John Gerstner, *The Evangelicals*, David F. Wells and John D. Woodbridge, eds. (Nashville: Abingdon Press, 1975), 23. See also Donald Bloesch, *Essentials of Evangelical Theology*, Vol. I (New York: Harper & Row, 1978), 7.

3. Littell, Franklin H., *The Anabaptist View of the Church* (Boston: Starr King Press, 1958), 12. See also Roland Bainton, *The Reformation of the Sixteenth Century* (Boston: Beacon Press, 1952), 68. It would be well at this point to note that the Anabaptist movement that sprang up from within the Reformation is not to be identified with the English Baptist movement which originated at a somewhat later time. The Anabaptist movement has issued in such groups as the Mennonites and the Amish. The English Baptist movement has issued in such groups as the American Baptist Convention and the Southern Baptist Convention.

4. Bainton, *The Reformation of the Sixteenth Century*, 60-61.

5. Montgomery, ed., *God's Inerrant Word*, 264-265.

6. J. H. Merle D'Aubigne, *History of the Reformation*, Vol. I (New York: American Tract Society), 163.

7. Williston Walker, *A History of the Christian Church*, rev. ed. (New York: Charles Scribner's Sons, 1959), 125.

8. W. H. C. Frend, *The Rise of Christianity* (Philadelphia: Fortress Press, 1984), 54.

9. D'Aubigne, *History of the Reformation*, 195-196.

10. John M. Todd, *Martin Luther* (New York: Paulist Press, 1964), 78.

11. Frend, *The Rise of Christianity*, 54.

12. Eusebius, *The History of the Christian Church: From Christ to Constantine*, G. A. Williamson, trans. (Harmondsworth, Middlesex, England: Dorset Press, 1965), 137.

13. In a later chapter we will discuss the meaning and significance of the ethical teachings of Jesus as they were perceived by the post-resurrection Apostolic Church.

14. F. F. Bruce, *The Books and the Parchments* (Westwood, N.J.: Fleming H. Revell Company, 1950), 9.

15. William Ragsdale Canon, *The Theology of John Wesley* (New York: Abingdon Press), 63.

16. Ibid., 40-41.

17. Ibid., 38.

18. Ibid., 63.

19. Vivian H. H. Green, *The Young Mr. Wesley* (New York: St. Martin's Press, 1961), 50.

20. Canon, *The Theology of John Wesley*, 72.

21. John Wesley was very much a Catholic in his views on sex and human sexuality. Thus celibacy was considered the most "spiritual" of states for one seeking perfection. In addition, he was a fellow of Lincoln College with a guaranteed annual stipend as long as he did not marry.

22. John Wesley's Journal, Friday, 2 December 1757.

23. Albert Outler, ed., *John Wesley* (New York: Oxford University Press, 1964), 65.

24. John Wesley's Journal, Wednesday, 24 May 1738.

25. Martin Luther, Preface to Romans.

26. John Wesley's Journal, Sunday, 4 June 1738.

27. Hermeneutics is the task of biblical interpretation. A paradigm is a structure, by which other relevant facts and ideas are understood and interpreted.

28. Albert C. Outler, *Theology in the Wesleyan Spirit* (Nashville: Discipleship Resources-Tidings, 1975), 36-37.

29. Outler, ed., *John Wesley*, 209.

30. Ibid., 59. Any doubts about Wesley's oneness with the *sole fide* doctrine of the Reformation ought to be removed by this passage.

31. Franz Hildebrandt, *From Luther to Wesley* (London: Lutterworth Press, 1951), 23.

Chapter Three

Anabaptism and Evangelicalism

K enneth Kantzer has stated that the two fundamental principles of the Reformation that form the basis of modern Evangelicalism are: 1) Justification occurs at the beginning of the Christian life through faith in Christ; and 2) Scripture illuminated by the Holy Spirit is the only trustworthy guide in matters of faith and practice.[1]

It is a thesis of this study that defining the essentials of historic Evangelicalism by these two principles alone *is not enough*. At no point does this become more clear than in a study of the Protestant Reformation and what is often incorrectly referred to as the Radical Reformation.

The Challenge of Anabaptism

In the wake of the success of Luther and Zwingli in breaking with the Catholic church, another movement emerged. The movement is technically known as Anabaptism. The term Anabaptist derives from the cardinal doctrine that distinguished this movement from the other movements of reform in Germany and Switzerland. Anabaptism stated that the baptism of infants was invalid. Since all had been baptized and christened in the Catholic church, this meant that all must be rebaptized. It also meant that the practice of infant baptism should be stopped. The rite of baptism should be administered only to believing adults.[2]

To avoid confusion, let it be noted that continental Anabaptism is *not* to be identified with the English Baptist movement. While continental Anabaptism may have slightly influenced the English Baptist movement, the two have differing geographical origins and took differing forms. Anabaptism has issued in such modern denominations as the Mennonites and the Amish. The English Baptist movement has issued in such groups as the American and Southern Baptist Conventions.[3]

Anabaptism, as we shall see, taught that following the ethical teachings and the example of Jesus (as in Roman Catholic monasticism) was of primary soteriological significance, rather than simple trusting faith in the finished work of Jesus' crucifixion and resurrection, as in Pauline and Apostolic soteriology. Because of their emphasis on justification by faith alone, the English Baptists and their descendants are in the mainstream of historic "Evangelical" theology and soteriology.

The Anabaptist movement originated from within the matrix of the continental Reformation. The principle of biblical authority over the authority of popes and councils was appealed to in Anabaptism as it had been by the Reformers. But as the Reformation progressed, the Anabaptists, though thoroughgoing Protestants in the sense of protesting the alleged abuses of the Catholic church, emerged as a distinct and even antagonistic movement to that of the Evangelicals or Reformers.

Early disputes between the Anabaptist leadership and the Reformers centered largely around the question of infant baptism. But we must not make the mistake of thinking that this was the only or even the key issue. As Anabaptism progressed, it showed a distinct affinity for *the ethical teachings and example of the earthly Jesus* as the content and means of salvation rather than faith in His death and resurrection as the sole ground of salvation, as in Paul. There was considerable unanimity of belief among the various groups that it was in following the teachings of Jesus (especially the Sermon on the Mount), and copying the simple lifestyle of our Lord, that the essence of Christianity was to be found.

Salvation in Anabaptism

Church historian William Packull, in commenting on the soteriology of one of Anabaptism's most influential thinkers, Hans Denck, says that Denck, like all Anabaptists, saw redemption to be more in following Christ as a human example than in believing in the finished work of Christ on the cross.[4]

Of another influential Anabaptist leader Packull observes, "Hut believed that Christ's conception, birth, passion, and resurrection were to be repeated in every true follower of Jesus."[5] Salvation was thus conceived in terms of ethical response rather than simple trust and faith. That the Anabaptists showed an implicit aversion to the writings and theology of Paul seems clear in the following statement of Menno Simons. "The true evangelical faith," said he, "sees and considers *only the doctrine, ceremonies, commands, prohibitions, and the perfect example of Christ,* and strives to conform thereto with all its power" (italics mine).[6]

We have previously seen that monasticism, which eventually gave rise to Roman Catholicism, emerged as a direct result of shifting from the theology and soteriology of Paul to attempting to follow the teachings of the earthly Jesus. Therefore, except on the question of infant baptism, we see that Anabaptism is ideologically far closer to Catholic theology than to the theology of the Reformers. Packull comments, "The whole first generation of Anabaptist leaders came not out of the halls of Wittenberg but out of the halls of Roman Catholicism. They represent not a further, more complete reform, as they do so often insist, but the elevation of Catholic mysticism . . ."[7]

Authority in Anabaptism

As the Anabaptist positions began to be questioned, opposition to them arose. Many fled to Basel where the great Catholic humanist Erasmus was writing and teaching.[8] Bainton observes,

> There were three elements in Erasmus' position which the radicals could appropriate. The first was the way in which he envisaged the restoration of primitive Christianity. The central point for him was not, as for Luther, the doctrine of justification by faith, but the

pattern of New Testament behavior, the exemplifica-
tion of the Sermon on the Mount, the literal imitation
of Christ. The second point was aversion to dogma,
whether cold from Rome or hot from Wittenberg.
"Deeds are more important than creeds. . . ."[9] The third
principle was inwardness, the spirit against the flesh
and the spirit against the letter.[10]

This last point deserves some consideration. Catholic
mystics and Anabaptists felt that the immediate revelation
of the Holy Spirit, unmediated by doctrines or the
Scriptures, was of more authority than Scripture itself.
Thus when we say that "Scripture illumined by the Holy
Spirit is the only trustworthy guide in matters of faith and
practice,"[11] we must be very careful to distinguish between
the Reformation position on pneumatology[12] and the
Catholic and Anabaptist position.

The Catholic church believed, as did the Anabaptists,
in the authority of ongoing revelation and inspiration.
They gave it an authority equal to that of Scripture. Thus
if it seemed correct to the Catholic Magisterium that since,
on their viewpoint, justification did not occur until the
end of life's journey or near its end, and many would never
find it in this life, there must be an intermediate place of
purgation for those who died Catholics, but not perfected
Catholics. They believed the Holy Spirit had led them to
the necessity of a purgatory. Certain apocryphal verses of
Scripture were then brought in after the fact in support.

The similarity of Anabaptist pneumatology and the
hermeneutical methodology of Catholicism can be clearly
seen in Anabaptism's position concerning pacifism. Early
in Anabaptist history, the Old Testament Scriptures

pertaining to the use of violence for the establishment of the kingdom of God on this earth were appealed to in fanatical fashion by Thomas Müntzer, Jan Leyden, and a host of others. Their desire to establish the kingdom led to the feeling that the Holy Spirit was directing them to do so. Having decided that the Holy Spirit was so leading, all the Scriptures in favor of violence as a means to this end were adduced. Only after Müntzer's prophecies and Leyden's kingdom were brutally suppressed by superior forces did the Holy Spirit "lead" the Anabaptist "prophets" to elevate what is now considered to be one of their cardinal doctrines, that of absolute pacifism.[13] Thus the Anabaptist position on pacifism represents an interpretation based more on tradition grounded in experience rather than on Scripture.

The emphasis on the immediacy of "the word" through inner revelation and inner light as opposed to seeking revelation in the objective and authoritative Word of God contained in the Scriptures is everywhere apparent. "The theory that the Bible, interpreted by the inward light, was the only rule of faith, before which all human authority and institutions must bend, was now proclaimed with greater emphasis than ever . . ."[14] Not only was the inner light or word (synonymous with the Holy Spirit) the means of interpreting Scripture, it was *above* Scripture. Some were so certain of the lack of the necessity of Scripture because of the direct authority of the Holy Spirit in the form of revelation, that they burned their Bibles.[15]

While seldom pointed out, this was a huge point of difference between Luther, Zwingli, and the Anabaptists. All were claiming the authority of Scripture as illumined by the Holy Spirit. However, the Reformers insisted that the

Holy Spirit was revealed *only by the Word*, and the Word only by the Spirit. When someone once attempted to bring to Thomas Müntzer's attention that what he was proclaiming as a prophetic revelation was contrary to the written Word, he expostulated, "Bible, bibble, bauble . . ." Claiming a higher revelation than the Scriptures through the Spirit, Müntzer sought a dialogue with Martin Luther. The Reformer replied that he would not converse with Müntzer apart from the Scriptures even if he had swallowed the Holy Ghost, feathers and all!

Thus in discussing Evangelical hermeneutics, an important consideration must be added. The Word illumines the Spirit and the Spirit illumines the Word, but the objective Word is absolutely necessary and of primary importance to proper illumination by the Spirit, and not *vice versa*. In Paul's words: "Faith comes from hearing, and hearing by the word of Christ" (Romans 10:17, NASB). The Anabaptists with their hordes of prophets saw correctly that the Holy Spirit illumined Moses apart from any previously written word. But Luther saw correctly that false prophets have also flourished in every age. The writers of Scripture have undergone the test of time for the true and false prophet. The prophet of the moment cannot be tested, save through the canonical Scriptures and through "rightly dividing" this word of truth.

How Sinful Is Mankind?

One more important difference emerged between the Reformers (Evangelicals) and the Anabaptists. It lay in the difference in their anthropologies. The Anabaptists, with their emphasis on the primacy of the inner word or inner light, were mystics. Classical Christian mysticism suggests that though man is sinful, enough of the divine remains nascent within that one may be able to respond to God directly without the mediation of the external and objective Word.

In sharp contrast, the Reformers taught the Pauline doctrine of the absolute fallenness of man. In Adam all have died (1 Corinthians 15:22). We are enemies of God by nature (Colossians 1:21). We cannot save ourselves (Ephesians 2:5). We are without God (Ephesians 2:12). We need a Word from outside ourselves that will quicken and convince us to seek a Savior. Historic Evangelicalism from Luther to Wesley has seen the radical nature of justification solely by faith as the necessary corollary to the terribleness and completeness of the Fall.

The reason the Anabaptists never developed a doctrine of human depravity necessitating a radical doctrine of justification by faith seems to center in two things. First, most of them were quite untrained in theology and biblical exegesis. Anabaptism was basically a lay movement. They had the Scriptures that the Reformers had translated, but they did not have the previous judgments and interpretations that had been placed upon them through history. In sharp contrast to this, Luther and the Reformers, as well as Wesley, were skilled students of patristic literature as well as having been formally trained in theology. It is of some significance that the most highly trained leader of the Anabaptist movement, Beltthassar Hubmaier, agreed with Zwingli on virtually every point, including the primacy of Paul's writings. The main point of contention between the two lay in the question of infant baptism. Hubmaier's martyrdom left a leadership vacuum that was filled by men of considerably less ability.[16]

The second cause of the Anabaptists' lack of doctrine of the universal fallenness of man was their disdain of doctrines of any form. For them Christianity consisted not of doctrines, but of ethical activism. In this they clearly showed their preference for the Gospels and the teachings of the earthly Jesus. The Reformers (Evangelicals), including Wesley, showed a marked preference for the writings and theology of Paul, as did the earliest church.[17]

The foregoing discussion should demonstrate a most important point concerning the nature of historic Evangelicalism. To the doctrines of justification solely by faith, and the sole authority of Scripture in matters of faith and practice, must be added the Pauline doctrine of the total depravity of all mankind. Only when mankind lies fallen in the dust in utter humility—whether a proud Pharisee on the road to Damascus, or a humbled Anglican churchman utterly defeated and retreating homeward from Georgia to England—only then can one see clearly that mankind everywhere is not primarily in need of an example, but of a Savior. This is the heart of historic Christianity. And it is the heart of classical Evangelicalism.

Summing Up

Historic Evangelicalism was born during the Reformation through the rediscovery and reassertion of the *sola fide* soteriology of the apostle Paul by Martin Luther. Luther was an Augustinian monk, and it is of great significance that the chief architect of the recovery of the primitive church's outlook on the nature of salvation should have come from within the very movement (monastic) that had caused the break from the purity and simplicity of the Apostolic message. The Reformers, as well as John

Wesley, concurred on the primacy of Pauline anthropology and soteriology.

In contrast, Anabaptism and the monastic movement elevated the ethical teachings and example of the earthly Jesus as a model to be followed for salvation.

The time has come to raise the question—which viewpoint is correct?

Notes

1. Kenneth Kantzer, *The Evangelicals*, Wells and Woodbridge, eds., 38.

2. Williston Walker, *A History of the Christian Church*, rev. ed. (New York: Charles Scribner's Sons, 1959), 326-332.

3. William R. Estep, *The Anabaptist Story* (Nashville: Broadman Press, 1963), 200-201.

4. William O. Packull, *Mysticism and the Early South German Christian Anabaptist Movement 1525-1530* (Scottsdale, Penn.: Herald Press, 1977), 49. Some modern manifestations of the Mennonite movement such as the Mennonite Brethren in Christ, show a much closer affinity theologically to mainstream Evangelicalism than do the more traditional Anabaptist groups that still follow the viewpoint of early Anabaptist leadership. (See *Christianity Today*, 5 March 1990.)

5. Ibid., 68.

6. Walter Klassen, *Anabaptism: Neither Catholic nor Protestant* (Waterloo, Ontario: Contrad Press, 1973), 20.

7. Packull, *Mysticism*, 176.

8. Franklin H. Littell, *The Anabaptist View of the Church* (Boston: Starr King Press, 1958), 12.

9. The cry of "deeds not creeds" is one of the hallmarks of liberalism and of the New Evangelical Left. The leadership in the New Evangelical Left has taken sixteenth-century Anabaptist methodology and hermeneutics and sold it to the Evangelical movement as being part and parcel of Evangelicalism. Historically Anabaptism and Evangelicalism were two separate and distinct movements within Protestantism. The distinctions persist to this day and need to be recovered by the Evangelical community if it is not to drift off into the soteriological errors of Anabaptism—errors perceived by Luther, Zwingli, Calvin, and at a later time by John Wesley.

10. Roland Bainton, *The Reformation of the Sixteenth Century* (Boston: Beacon Press, 1952), 69. That the Anabaptists received ideological aid from a staunch Roman Catholic like Erasmus raises the question of just how theologically reformed they really were. On this point see also A. C. McGiffert, *A History of Christian Thought*, Vol. II (New York, Scribners, 1950), 392-393.

11. Kantzer, *The Evangelicals*, 38.

12. Pneumatology is the study of the doctrine of the Holy Spirit. Roman Catholicism believes that the Holy Spirit continues to reveal truth through the magisterium. This truth can be as authoritative, or

even more authoritative, than Scripture. Anabaptist mysticism allowed for authoritative ongoing revelation also, but since they never organized as a group the authority was given to individual prophets.

13. Albert H. Newman, *A Manual of Church History*, Vol. II (Chicago: The American Baptist Publication Society, 1931), 178.

14. E. Befort Bax, *The Rise and Fall of the Anabaptists* (American Scholar Publications, 1966), 4.

15. Ibid., 59.

16. Estep, *The Anabaptist Story*, 84-85.

17. The question of the importance of the theology of Paul to historic Evangelicalism is not in dispute. As this study progresses, it will be demonstrated that the Apostolic Age as well as the Patristic period was also dominated by the theological and ethical judgments of Paul. The Anabaptist declension from the primacy of the Pauline understandings constituted a serious difference between the Anabaptists and the Reformers and caused both the Reformers and the Anabaptists to see themselves as separate and distinct movements.

Chapter Four

Jesus and the Old Covenant

I t should be clear that there is a distinct difference in the issues addressed in the ministry of Jesus and the issues that occupied Paul and the Apostolic church. F. F. Bruce observes,

> Scholars have noted on the one hand complete lack of material in the Gospels on such a burning issue of the Apostolic Church as circumcision, or the charismatic gifts which loomed so large in some of Paul's churches. Little is included on baptism, the Gentile mission, the food laws, or church-state relations. . . . On the other hand, the synoptic Gospels abound in teaching on the Son of man and the kingdom of God

(which were apparently little stressed in the apostolic church) and give prominence to Jesus' controversies with the Pharisees on the Sabbath observance and the corban question, which do not seem to be live issues at a later period.[1]

It is at this point that one of the most critical issues in New Testament interpretation is raised. How shall we account for these differences?

Some have gone so far as to suggest that the Apostolic church erroneously followed the teachings of Paul and should have instead followed the teachings of Jesus.[2] But that, in turn, creates tremendous additional problems. For it can be demonstrated that those things which made Christianity unique from Judaism are not to be found in the teachings of Jesus, but in the instructions of Paul. If the New Testament were to end with the Gospel of John, we should know nothing of any real significance concerning the laying aside of the rite of circumcision or the seating of men and women together in Paul's churches as equals and "heirs together of eternal life," a custom which broke totally with the synagogue custom of gender segregation—a custom not challenged by the earthly Jesus. We should have virtually no doctrine of the church and precious little of New Testament soteriology. Without Acts and the epistles, the Gospels alone would never lead us to those things which make Christianity unique.

How then shall we understand the life and teachings of Jesus in relationship to the rest of the New Testament?

Interpretive Challenges

The prospective interpreter of the New Testament faces many problems. To begin with, because the Gospels have traditionally been placed at the front of the New Testament, they are read as though they chronologically follow the Old Testament documents. But of course, this is untrue.

The first written documents accepted without question by the earliest, or Apostolic, church were the epistles of Paul. Paul's epistles do not represent the judgment of just one faction of the Apostolic church, as is so often inferred. He wrote nothing (at least nothing that we have) until after the Jerusalem Council (A.D. 49). And it was here at Jerusalem that "the pillars," the Aramaic-speaking wing of the Apostolic church, agreed with Paul that the central issue of Christian soteriology is justification solely by faith in Christ (Acts 15:11).

The epistles of Paul which are primarily doctrinal in nature represent the consensus of the Apostolic church gathered. They also represent the first New Testament documents that were considered authoritative. One would be hard pressed to disagree with Hebrew scholar Hyam Maccoby's pungent observation, "Paul is, in a sense, present from the very first word of the New Testament."[3] While it was necessary from an informational standpoint to place the Gospels at the front of the New Testament writings (just who is this Jesus, anyway?), the epistles of Paul represent the doctrinal and hermeneutical assumptions of the Apostolic community. This means that the Gospels must be read in the light of the epistles (as Luther correctly perceived), and not *vice versa*.[4]

A second problem that confronts the prospective interpreter of the New Testament is the question of where the Old Covenant ends and the New begins. While it seems clear that justification always has been by faith under both covenants (Hebrews 11, Romans 4), it also seems quite clear that there are some significant differences between the Old and New Covenants. The Old was found to have flaws. The New is based on better promises and a better sacrifice and is ministered to believers not by a human priestly class, but by the Holy Spirit (Hebrews 8 and 9; Romans 8). Further, even as the prophetic voice of the Old Testament had predicted the coming of Messiah, so it had predicted the coming of a New and better Covenant (Jeremiah 31:31-34). The question becomes: When did the Old Covenant end and the New begin?

When we turn to that portion of the Bible that begins with Matthew's Gospel, we read the bold slogan, NEW TESTAMENT. Thus the tendency is to read all that follows as though it took place under the New Covenant. A little reflection will reveal that this cannot be correct.

Jeshua

It is Paul who reminds us that Jesus was born under the Law (Galatians 4:4). That long-ago night in Bethlehem, Mary fondly gave her firstborn a very Jewish name, *Jeshua*—the Aramaic equivalent of the Hebrew Joshua. But unlike Joshua who had been a political deliverer, Jeshua's deliverance was to be not political but spiritual: "He will save His people from their sins" (Matthew 1:21). From His circumcision and Mary's purification according to the Law (Luke 2:21-24), Jesus' entire pre-resurrection existence was lived out under the Law.

His dispute with the Pharisees about the Sabbath and Sabbatarian regulations was not a dispute over the institution of the Sabbath, but about certain traditions that some (not all)[5] of the rabbis had generated which were hindering its intended function (Luke 3:11-17). Jesus instructed the leper whom He had just healed to go and show himself to the priest and offer the gift proscribed by the Law (Matthew 8:1-3). His crucifixion was the result of applying the penalty of the Mosaic Law for asserting that He was the Son of God (Mark 14:16-64). It is of enormous significance that this was the *only* charge of breach with the Mosaic Law that was corroborated at His trial indicating that He had indeed kept the law at every point. His resurrection substantiated His characterization of Himself as uniquely God's Son.

Thus one of the most important factors in New Testament interpretation begins to present itself: Jesus of Nazareth, from the human and historical standpoint, was fully a Jew, and He was conscious He was living out His life under the authority of the Old Covenant, of which the Law was the foundation.

At first this appears so obvious that it seems unnecessary to consider. But in point of fact, centuries of anti-semitism and centuries of identification with Western culture have resulted in a Jesus which is quite un-Jewish. This becomes most obvious in some of the famous paintings which have Jesus with blue eyes or fair hair (or both). While this error of an acculturated Christ is being vigorously exposed by the left wing of American Protestantism, it does not seem to have occurred to some of them that the fully human Jesus of history was Himself the product of first-century Hebrew acculturation.

Jesus the Jew

In his book, *The Jewish Reclamation of Jesus*, Fuller Seminary professor Donald Hagner writes, "The fact that

Jesus of Nazareth, the Christ of Christianity, was fully a Jew is increasingly recognized in our day." He goes on to say,

> It is rightly insisted on nowadays that in every regard the upbringing of Jesus was Jewish. He was born of Jewish parents in the homeland of the Jews, circumcised according to Jewish custom, and dedicated in the temple; he received the education of the Jewish child in Torah, became *bar mitzvah* at the age of thirteen, and—as we have every reason to believe—passed into manhood faithfully practicing his religion in both deed and word, as well as regular attendance in the synagogue.[6]

This full Jewishness of Jesus does not end with His lifestyle. In the main, His teaching and preaching reflects, both in form and content, the understanding and learning of His time. "His teaching indeed is very Jewish in tone, and it is quite possible as one reads his words to imagine that one is listening to a member of the great prophetic tradition of Israel, an Amos or an Isaiah."[7]

Not only did Jesus live His life out under the Law, but He was viewed as a teacher of the Law, a rabbi (John 1:38,49; 3:2,26; 6:25). Because of the Diaspora (the scattering of Jews across the world), there were Jewish enclaves in a large percentage of the cities and towns of the Roman empire. Because most of these cities were at some distance from Jerusalem, the Jewish population was effectively cut off from temple worship. In this situation of isolation from Jerusalem, they developed their own places of worship and instruction in the Scriptures. These became known as synagogues.

Each synagogue had its own rabbi or rabbis. The rabbi had gone beyond others in learning and studying the Scriptures and legal questions. Any Jewish male, regardless of birth or social standing, might become a rabbi if he was willing to pay the price of extended learning. Jesus' manner of preaching and teaching, and the material that He used, were clearly in the rabbinical tradition of the time.[8] "Even his quaint expressions such as 'a camel going through the eye of a needle,' or 'take the beam out of your own eye' are Pharisee locutions found in the Talmud."[9] Jewish scholar J. Klausner concludes that "there is not a single *ethical sentence* [italics mine] in the whole of the New Testament which cannot be paralleled either in the Old Testament, in the literature of the Apocrypha and Pseudipigrapha, or in the Talmud and Midrashic literature of the era of Jesus and Paul."[10]

In addition to coming to His own as a rabbi, Jesus came to His own as a prophet.[11] His rejection in the synagogue of Nazareth prompted Him to remark that no prophet is without honor except in his own country and among his own relations. He went on to liken His calling to that of Elijah and Elisha (Luke 4:24-27). That He convinced a great many that He was a prophet of considerable stature seems clear from the answer He received from the disciples to the question, "Whom do men say that I the Son of Man am?" They answered, "Some say that thou art John the Baptist: some, Elias; and others, Jeremias or one of the prophets" (Matthew 16:13-14, KJV). That He considered Himself to be the last of the prophets that would be sent to Israel under the Old Covenant seems clear also (Matthew 23:29-39; Luke 13:32-33).

The Sermon on the Mount

The particular teaching of Jesus that has assumed especial prominence for Christians and Christian interpreters of the

New Testament is the Sermon on the Mount. This teaching of Jesus is at once the basis for much of the Christian social action agenda and the absolute pacifism of both Anabaptists and Quakers. It looms large also in Roman Catholicism—especially in the monastic movement.

But when subjected to an analysis of the historical situation in which it was uttered, some rather startling things are revealed. Instead of the highly unique ethical statement that it has been thought to have been, we find that it is quite simply a reorganization and restatement of Hebrew Scripture and rabbinical literature and comment.

The beginning of the Sermon on the Mount, "Blessed are you who are poor," or "Blessed are the poor in spirit" (Luke 6:20; Matthew 5:3), is not some special blessing for a particular social class that springs fresh from the lips of Jesus.[12] F. C. Grant has pointed out (along with others) that the beginning of the Sermon on the Mount echoes and reflects the whole "poverty-piety" equation of the Old Testament and ancient Hebrew literature. "Indeed, the background of the Beatitudes as a whole (and of the Sermon on the Mount, and the whole of the ethical teaching of Jesus) is not merely the social-economic conditions prevailing in Palestine after the war against Rome . . . but the religion of the Old Testament; especially of the Psalms."[13]

It was the fact that Jesus was clearly claiming an authority from within Himself rather than an authority based on rabbinical ordination that raised eyebrows. He spoke as one "having authority." Since the authority was not from the proper accrediting agencies of His nation, it was a claim to the authority of the prophet—a direct authority from God.

Ultimately this claim to direct authority from God would be seen as an identification with God; and it was this claim, the claim to be the Son of God, that would bring about His crucifixion (Mark 14:60-62).

But if the Sermon on the Mount has been the source of much interest to Christian interpreters, it has become even more so to modern Hebrew scholars. It is just here that Jesus shows Himself more clearly than any other place in His teachings to be (in the words of another rabbi) "a Hebrew of the Hebrews."[14] Jesus' statement, "Do not think that I have come to abolish the Law or the Prophets; I have not come to abolish them but to fulfill them"—a statement from within the Sermon on the Mount (Matthew 5:17)—was a pronouncement that delighted the heart of the most stern and conservative first-century rabbi.

The point of all this is that the Sermon on the Mount does not in any way reflect some new and higher ethic of a great religious teacher, as difficult as this may be for some to accept. Rather, it represents the application of the Mosaic Law with all of its rigors. In the Sermon on the Mount, the listener of that time (as well as the reader of today) is not being turned forward to that which makes Christianity unique, but backward to orthodox Judaism. No one has appreciated this point more fully than C. S. Lewis, who has written:

> The idea . . . that Christianity brought a new ethical code into the world is a grave error. If it had done so, then we should have to conclude that all who first preached it wholly misunderstood their own message: for all of them its Founder, His Precursor, His Apostles, came demanding repentance and offering

forgiveness, a demand and an offer both meaningless except on the assumption of a moral law already known and already broken.[15]

In his book, *The Sermon on the Mount: The Modern Quest for Its Meaning*, Clarence Bauman says that New Testament scholar Hans Windisch has conclusively demonstrated that the *sitz im leben* of the Sermon on the Mount "stands entirely within the context of the Old Testament and of Judaism."[16] John Wesley defined preaching the Sermon on the Mount as preaching "the law."[17]

We therefore conclude that Jeshua came first to His own people as a rabbi and as the last of the prophets that operated under the assumptions of the Old Covenant. His manner of preaching is clearly rabbinical and prophetic. Outside of the parables and the few teachings that self-evidently apply specifically to the church (i.e. Matthew 16:13-20; 18:15-20) and anticipate its formation, there is nothing new or esoteric in the ethical teachings of Jesus.

The Cross at the Center

The uniqueness of Jesus does not lie in His teachings. Rather, it lies in His Being: His virgin birth, His sinless life, His atoning sacrificial death, and most especially His resurrection.

That this is where the Apostolic Church perceived Jesus' uniqueness to have its greatest significance seems clear from the paucity of references to His teachings from Acts onward. In contrast, witness the amount of references to His death and resurrection. Even the Synoptics, which were written to preserve biographical information, give an extraordinary amount of attention to those events that culminated in His death and resurrection—events that have been subsumed under the rubric, "the passion of Christ."

Jesus was not declared to be the Son of God because of His teachings. He was declared to be the Son of God with authority over all things by His resurrection (Matthew 28:18; Romans 1:3-4).

The centerpiece of Christianity is not the Sermon on the Mount; it is the resurrection of Christ.

Notes

1. F. F. Bruce, *History, Criticism, and Faith*, Colin Brown, ed. (Downers Grove, Ill.: Inter-Varsity Press, 1977), 125.

2. Hyam Maccoby, *The Mythmaker* (New York: Harper & Row, 1987). Jewish scholars are not the only ones who draw this conclusion. Protestant writers such as A. Schweitzer and R. Bultmann have leaned in the same direction.

3. Ibid., 4.

4. In the book *The Gospel According to Jesus* (Grand Rapids, Mich.: Zondervan Publishing Company, 1988), evangelical author John McArthur, Jr., bases his whole book on the mistaken assumption that "the Gospels are the foundation on which the epistles build" (p. 214).

5. Maccoby, *The Mythmaker*, 33-34.

6. Donald Hagner, *The Jewish Reclamation of Jesus* (Grand Rapids, Mich.: Zondervan Publishing Company, 1984), 21.

7. Ibid., 22.

8. Maccoby, *The Mythmaker*, 19-44.

9. Ibid., 44.

10. Hagner, *The Jewish Reclamation of Jesus*, 167. For a more complete discussion of the nature and sources of Jesus' teaching as a rabbi, see Asher Finkel, *The Pharisees and the Teacher of Nazareth* (Leiden, Netherlands: Leiden/Koln, 1964), 155-175.

11. W. H. C. Frend, *The Rise of Christianity* (Philadelphia: Fortress Press, 1984), 39.

12. Liberation theologians would have us believe that as a social class the "poor" are God's people without faith or conversion, and that somehow God's favor rests uniquely upon them. This view conveniently overlooks the extreme wealth of such important figures as Abraham, Isaac, Jacob, and David.

13. Frederick C. Grant, *An Introduction to New Testament Thought* (Nashville: Abingdon Press), 198.

14. Hagner, *The Jewish Reclamation of Jesus*, 88.

15. C. S. Lewis, *Christian Reflections*, Walter Hooper, ed. (Grand Rapids, Mich.: William B. Eerdmans Publishing Company, 1967), 46.

16. Clarence Bauman, *The Sermon on the Mount: The Modern Quest for Its Meaning* (Macon, Ga.: Mercer University Press, 1985), 229.

17. *John Wesley*, ed. Albert Outler (New York: Oxford Press, 1964), 232.

Chapter Five

Jesus and the New Covenant

On the eve of His betrayal and death, Jesus took the Passover cup and said to His disciples, "This is my blood of the new covenant which is shed for many" (Mark 14:24; Matthew 26:28). In referring to the blood that He would shed on the following day as "my blood of the new covenant," Jesus indicated at least two things. First, the New Covenant that had been prophesied (Jeremiah 31:31-34) was about to become an accomplished reality. Second, it was the shedding of His blood that would inaugurate the New Covenant. Thus we may not date the New Covenant as either in force or operating before the crucifixion of Jesus.

Old vs. New

One of the mistakes that interpreters of the Bible often make is to so minimize the differences between the Old and New Covenants as to virtually suggest that there is no practical difference between the two. The writer of Hebrews in commenting on Jeremiah's prediction of the coming New Covenant made no such mistake. "By calling this covenant 'new,'" he writes, "he has made the first one obsolete" (Hebrews 8:13). The entire letter to the Hebrews carefully delineates the clear differences between the Old Covenant made with Israel, and the New Covenant made with church-age believers. The transitory nature of the first is contrasted with the permanent and eternal nature of the second. The superiority of the New over the Old is emphasized again and again.

In addition to the clear prediction of the prophets (especially Jeremiah) concerning the coming of a New Covenant, there was also the Jewish doctrine of two ages; "This Age" and "the Age to Come." "This Age" would be ruled by the Mosaic Law, the "Age to Come" by Messiah. In Galatians 1:4 Paul is clearly implying that "by virtue of the death (and resurrection) of Christ the boundary between the two ages is crossed, and those who believe belong no more to the present evil age, but to the glorious age to come," or the kingdom.[1]

The death and resurrection of Jesus and the descent of the Holy Spirit, while separate events, actually constitute one single event: the end of the Old Age and the dawning of the New.

The Change at Pentecost

Jesus had clearly warned the disciples at the Last Supper that they would not be able to properly understand and interpret all that they had seen and heard until the Holy Spirit would come to guide them into all truth (John 16:7-14). The prophets had characterized the New Age as an Age in which all flesh would be candidates for the Spirit of Yahweh. The Law of God would no longer be written on tablets of stone, but in the fleshy tables of the heart (Joel 2:28-29; Jeremiah 31:34). Thus, both from the standpoint of the prophetic tradition and from the teaching of Jesus at the Last Supper, the New Covenant could not be fully inaugurated before the descent of the Spirit.

F. F. Bruce observes, "The outpouring of the Spirit and the coming of the kingdom of God are two different ways of viewing the ministry of Jesus; both are manifested in partial measure before his death, but only after his death—his being 'glorified,' in Johannine terminology—will the kingdom come with power, will the Spirit be poured out in fulness . . . The putting of God's Spirit within men was a sign of the new covenant . . ."[2] The disciples had at last become believers in the full New Testament sense.

Further, the rabbinical doctrine of the ages, culminating in the final or Messianic Age, was understood by Peter to have found fulfillment on the day of Pentecost: "This is what was spoken by the prophet Joel: In the last days I will pour out my Spirit on all my people" (Acts 2:16-17). The "last days" clearly refers to the final age that the prophets had foretold. Thus Peter indicates that the fulfillment of this important prophecy was taking place on that day, the day of Pentecost. It is not to be looked forward to merely as some special outpouring that will mark the end of the age, but is a sign of the inauguration of the final or Messianic Age. Significantly, this is the last time in the New Testament that the Old Testament prophecy is appealed to as having an *immediate* fulfillment.[3]

This means that the apostles saw the day of Pentecost as not only the birthday of the church, but also as the beginning of their journey as people of the New Covenant. They had been *with* Jesus. Now they were "in Christ," as "new creations;" old things had passed away and all things were new (2 Corinthians 5:17).

Peter's defense of his evangelization of the Gentile Cornelius makes it plain that the disciples believed their full understanding of and identification with the New Covenant began with the outpouring of the Holy Spirit on the day of Pentecost. When "called on the carpet" before the entire assembly for his unorthodox behavior, he paired the outpouring of the Spirit on the household of Cornelius with that which occurred on the day of Pentecost: "And as I began to speak, the Holy Ghost fell on them as on us *at the beginning*"[4] (Acts 11:15, italics mine). Peter's use of the inclusive "us" indicates that there was agreement among the group that Pentecost represented the inauguration or beginning of the New Age. John Wesley was correct that "the disciples themselves had not the proper Christian faith till after the day of Pentecost."[5]

The disciples who had waited for the descent of the Holy Spirit now once again begin to move boldly. Their Master who had been with them, was now "in them" through His Spirit. Significantly, there are no long discussions based on the preaching and teaching of the earthly Jesus as to what they should do and teach. They are now aware of a direct and immediate leading of the risen and ascended Christ. Teaching gave way to proclamation (or *kerygma*). The sermons in the book of Acts, while exalting the role of Jesus as risen Savior and Lord, are virtually silent concerning His role as an earthly teacher of social ethics.

New Understandings

The descent of the promised Comforter had given rise to a new and cosmic understanding of who Christ was. The inauguration of the New Covenant and the New Age radically altered both their understanding of the kingdom and the means of its advance.

This was necessary because, for one thing, the gospel was now to be preached in all the world. The activity of Jesus as well as the prophets had taken place largely within the context of the nation of Israel and under its theonomous and historical assumptions. Now the gospel of the kingdom must be preached to people who have had no prior understanding of the meaning of a kingdom under the rule of Yahweh. For another, the gospel will now be proclaimed to audiences who are steeped in polytheism and paganism. The old wineskin of Judaism had burst and the new wine of the kingdom was flowing into all the world. New problems were being raised; new solutions would need to be found.

Differences Between the Old and New Covenants

Previously I have insisted that the differences between the Old Covenant and the New Covenant need to be magnified rather than minimized. The writer of Hebrews is especially adept at this task. His conclusion that the Old

Covenant contained a mere shadow of things to come (Hebrews 10:1) comes at the end of a long list of contrasts showing the New Covenant to be different and far superior to the Old in virtually all respects.

A little reflection turns up other differences that need our attention as well. Again, it must be pointed out that in the main these differences do not surface until after the death and resurrection of our Lord.

For example, when Jesus had sent His disciples on their preaching mission, it was with a specific and important geographical and religious limitation: "Go not into the way of the Gentiles . . . But go rather to the lost sheep of the house of Israel" (Matthew 10:5,6). After the resurrection Jesus says, "Go ye therefore, and teach all nations. . . ." (Matthew 28:19). Yet they were not to go until the Holy Spirit had descended to give them power and complete understanding (Luke 24:49; Acts 1:4-8). This lines up with Jesus' instruction in the farewell discourses of John's Gospel, in which Jesus indicated that although they had been eyewitness to everything, they would not be able to correctly interpret what they had seen and heard until the Holy Spirit had come to them (John 16:7-15). Having carefully followed Jesus' instructions and having received the Holy Spirit, they began moving out on their missions of proclamation.

But there was a problem. The only Scriptures they had at this time were the Scriptures of the Hebrew religion—the Scriptures of the Old Covenant. How might they extrapolate new solutions to new problems and beliefs from the old?

Scripture and the New Covenant

While it is self-evident that they solved the problem, it is the question of *how* they solved the problem that demands some attention. Of the Apostolic application and interpretation of the Old Covenant to the New Covenant situation, F. F. Bruce notes, "Here was the church's Bible. Here was the Bible of the Jewish people also; but so differently did the two communities read the same writings that, for practical purposes, they might have been using two different Bibles instead of sharing one."[6] Where did the apostles get this new interpretation—one that differed radically even from some of the understandings that they had held as Jesus' disciples?

It is at this point that one of the key problems of New Testament interpretation—the relationship of the teachings of the earthly Jesus to the teachings of the Apostolic community and especially the instructions of Paul—comes into focus. The apparent problem can be stated simply like this: Jesus was the Founder of the Christian faith; Paul was not. Should the teachings of Jesus assume a position of primary importance when teaching and interpreting the New Testament?

There is a straw man hidden in this equation that must be rooted out and destroyed. As previously noted, Jesus' personal existence did not end with the tomb in the garden of Joseph of Arimathea. He rose from the dead and ascended into heaven, there to continue through His Spirit to instruct His followers what His coming into time meant, as well as how to relate the Scriptures of the Old Covenant to that event. The "chosen vessel" for this task would be the apostle Paul.

Paul and the Gospel

As we study the New Testament on the calling and ministry of the apostle Paul, we become aware that if we are to take seriously the New Testament from the book of Acts onward, we must also take seriously Paul's place in the scheme of things. From his remarkable conversion and baptism to the end of his life, he was acutely aware of a unique relationship with the risen Christ. As we read of his conversion through a special appearance of the risen and ascended Lord, and of the special revelation that Ananias received regarding Paul as a "chosen vessel" as recorded by Luke (Acts 9), we are made aware of the awe with which the Apostolic community eventually regarded him. His gathered writings, the first canonical writings of the New Testament, were called simply, *The Apostle*.

Even though he received the gospel by direct revelation aside and apart from Apostolic tradition (Galatians 1:11-12), he was very careful to check his understandings with the apostles who had been eyewitnesses (Galatians 1 and 2). So sure was he of his Apostolic and authoritative position in the primitive church that at one point he "withstood Peter to his face" for teaching one thing and practicing another (Galatians 2:11-16).

Paul began most of his letters to the churches with a reminder that he, no less than Peter, James, and the others, is called by God's grace to be an apostle. He is able to distinguish between his own dominical rulings and those of the risen Christ (1 Corinthians 7:1-16). He is so confident that his teaching has the authority of Christ, he suggests that those who don't recognize his dominical authority should be regarded as unbelievers (Galatians 1:1-12). Even as Jesus had said to the disciples, "Follow me," Paul suggests that believers should follow him as he is following the Lord Himself (1 Corinthians 4:6; 11:1; 1 Thessalonians 1:6).

Paul had gone on from the synagogue to do post-graduate studies in Jerusalem under the most famous and respected rabbi of the first century, Gamaliel (Acts 22:3). Thus he became a Pharisee, a rabbi—one who had been instructed by the Hebrew sages. It is Paul who would be entrusted, not only with the Gentile mission and the evangelization of Asia Minor, but also with the task of framing and articulating the doctrines that would ultimately distinguish Christianity from Judaism.

Paul's Unique Perspective

C. H. Dodd has observed that "Paul was not only the first Christian theologian. He is also our earliest authority for the facts and beliefs upon which the Christian religion rests. He came in contact with the Christian tradition, through its original bearers, during the first decade after the Crucifixion. After that he had for many years little contact with the Aramaic-speaking wing of the Church, in which the Synoptic tradition grew up."[7]

Here Professor Dodd touches on several items which must always be a part of any responsible discussion concerning Pauline theology and Christian tradition. First, while not an eyewitness of the earthly Jesus (as far as can be determined), his writings form the earliest example of "those things which were most surely believed." His conversion to Christianity (not later than A.D. 34)[8] came only after he had had intimate, face-to-face, hostile contact with those early Christians as their persecutor and destroyer. It was not just Stephen's spirited defense (Acts 7) of the faith held by the earliest of Christians, but also countless other scenes similar in nature and content that were witnessed as Saul of Tarsus sought to stamp out Christianity. What these Christians believed they were willing to die for. Thus what they believed made an indelible impression upon their persecutor!

Following his conversion, Paul spent three years in Arabia before going to Jerusalem to confer with Peter and James. Then fourteen years later, he came back to Jerusalem with Barnabas, bringing with them a Gentile convert from Asia Minor named Titus. Paul discussed in some detail at this time the relevant theological and soteriological questions with the entire leadership of the Jerusalem church (Galatians 2:1-10).[9] If we accept A.D. 34 as the latest possible date for Paul's conversion, this means that the writing of his first epistle (1 Thessalonians) took place just after this historic consultation with the Christian leadership in Jerusalem.[10] The letters to Galatia and Corinth followed in quick succession.

It would seem then that Paul's triumph at the Jerusalem conference which took place in A.D. 49, established him in the eyes of the early church as being the person to whom their ecclesiastical and doctrinal questions should be brought. Paul's letters to the young churches are the result. He had met with "the pillars" of the mother church at Jerusalem. They had agreed that in substance their understandings of the nature of salvation were the same as his. Thus the Pauline tradition and the Apostolic Tradition are ONE.

The Gospel of the Judaizers

It is at this point that we pause to note that the term *euaggelion* from which the word "gospel" as well as the word "evangelical" come from, is a specifically Christian adaptation of the term "and as such was almost certainly developed by Paul within the early Christian community."[11] Of considerable importance is the fact that Paul and Mark were the first of the Christian writers to place the word *euaggelion* as "the good news of Jesus Christ" into writing. That he did so only after his initial conference with Peter, and later his meeting with the leaders of the Aramic speaking Jerusalem church (of which Matthew, Mark, and James were a part), indicates that Paul understood his perception of the meaning of the term "gospel" to be identical with the understandings of the writers of the synoptics.[12]

The significance of this for this study can begin to be appreciated when we read Paul's words to the Galatian Christians: "I am astonished that you are so quickly deserting the one who called you by the grace of Christ and are turning to a different gospel—which is really no gospel at all" (Galatians 1:6-7). Any student of New Testament history recognizes those who preached this "other gospel" which was no gospel at all as the Judaizers, later known as the Ebionites. Along with the Scriptures of the Old Testament, some of them came to accept only the Gospel of Matthew (with the Sermon on the Mount) and rejected all the writings of Paul.[13]

Because the Gospel of Matthew was not written until the middle of the seventh decade of the first century (A.D. 75), the Judaizers who were opposing Paul's early missionary work were using the Old Testament and the oral traditions of the sayings of Jesus. The fact that in their later Ebionite form they came to regard Matthew as the single canonical Scripture of the New Testament, would argue strongly that the oral tradition they had carried to Galatia was the oral tradition of those parts of the Sermon on the

Mount which carried Jesus' statement, "Think not that I have come to destroy the Law." The historic play-offs between the ethical teachings of Jesus and the teachings of Paul were almost certainly begun by the Judaizers.

This probable misuse and misinterpretation of the oral tradition of the Sermon on the Mount is perhaps why Paul wrote, "but even if we or an angel from heaven should preach a gospel other than the one we preached to you, let him be accursed" (Galatians 1:8). That the entire Apostolic community was in agreement with Paul on this matter is made clear from the outcome of the Jerusalem conference (Acts 15). That no one in the Apostolic community, including James, was involved in this misinterpretation of the function of ethical teachings of Jesus becomes clear as the Judaizers were branded by the apostles themselves as *those without Apostolic authorization* (Acts 15:24).

The First Christian Theologian

As "the first Christian theologian," Paul was called upon to articulate the distinctive doctrines of the Christian faith. The most important of these doctrines is the doctrine of justification solely by faith in the atonement of Christ.[14] The idea that individual faith constitutes the medium whereby one receives God's grace did not originate with Paul. It was an ancient biblical theme dating back to the story and experience of Abraham. The writer of Hebrews suggests that it goes back even further, to the experience of Abel, Enoch, and Noah (Hebrews 11:4-7).

The question of why God had chosen Israel to be His elect occupied much rabbinical discussion and generated varying viewpoints. While some schools of thought held that God had chosen Israel because of the merit of the

Exodus generation, others held that it was because of the merit of the patriarchs. Still others, like the school of Shamai, held that it was because of the merit of Abraham.[15]

At least two interesting points emerge from this discussion. The first is that the rabbis were divided in arguing individual merit vs. collective merit. The second is that it was the school of Shamai that was arguing for individual merit, specifically that of Abraham. The indication here is that while Paul had sat at the feet of Gamaliel, grandson of the famed Hillel, he had not closed his fertile mind to the cross pollination of ideas emerging from the rival school of Shamai. Well known is the marked difference between how Hillel liberalized the application and interpretation of the Torah with the hard-nosed literalism of the school of Shamai.

In finding Abraham as his model for doing biblical interpretation, Paul pointed out that it was not because of Abraham's merit that God chose him, but because of his response of faith to God's word. Thus the Christian soteriological system of individual faith found strong support in the Old Testament. Abraham becomes the father of all who enter the Covenant through faith (Romans 4). Following his Damascus road encounter, Paul knew that to enter the New Covenant, Christ was the object of that faith.

While the Old Covenant constantly addressed the salvation of Israel as a nation, we find the New Testament perceiving salvation as individual rather than collective. Where God dealt with a nation, now He deals with individuals. Thus we find Jesus calling the Twelve. Their occupations, names, and backgrounds are given. Paul's writings abound with the names of those who have heard the gospel and responded in faith: Timothy, Titus, Pricilla and Acquilla, Luke, Onesimus. It is individuals with names and faces who are redeemed; societies and nations are not.

Still, those redeemed as individuals now find a new identity as "the people of God," the "divine commonwealth" (1 Peter 2:9). One of Paul's many unique contributions to Christianity was the concept of *koinonia* or community. Greek and Oriental speculative systems had taught oneness with the divine, but they had never taught oneness with one another and community through spiritual bonds. Morton Scott Enslin notes, "In this field, Paul was a pioneer."[16] It is within the church, the "new Israel," that Paul sees the rule of God over a "chosen people" raising the ethical question. Brother must not go to law against brother (2 Corinthians 6:1-8). The Christian community, the *ekklesia*, is ordained of God. Therefore a new relationship is called for among its members (Ephesians 5:22-6:4).

The terms "brother" or "brethren" are used virtually exclusively throughout the New Testament to denote fellow believers of the household of faith. From the Gospel of Matthew where Jesus defines who His real mother, brothers, and sisters are (Matthew 12:46-50), through the writings of Paul and the apostles, the terms brother, brothers, or brethren are used to denote fellow believers of the household of faith.

Once again, let it be pointed out that inasmuch as Paul's writings are the first of our New Testament writings, and inasmuch as one of Paul's several unique contributions to Christian thought lies in his teaching of *koinonia* (as previously established), it is most likely that he is also the one who established the idea of brotherhood and family to describe the new relationship that believers have with one another through being children of God (Galatians 4:1-7).

In this regard let us further note that the New Testament introduces a clear distinction between "neighbor," and "brothers" and "sisters" in the Lord. "Neighbor" is used to designate anyone who is in proximity. While love of neighbor is called for from Leviticus (19:18) to the Apostolic church (Romans 13:9), there is a distinct and evident discrimination between the ethical responsibilities that Christians hold toward "the brethren" and those held toward a "neighbor."

This becomes especially clear in Paul's dominical ruling against marriage with an unbeliever. If being a "neighbor" was the only qualification for a suitable mate, then anyone in geographical proximity would qualify. But Paul says to qualify for marriage with a believer, one must be more than neighbor, one must also be a fellow believer. Therefore he writes, "Do not be yoked together with unbelievers . . . For what do righteousness and wickedness have in common? Or what fellowship can light have with darkness? What harmony is there between Christ and Belial? What does a believer have in common with an unbeliever" (2 Corinthians 6:14-18)?

No Social Engineering

Here again a distinction would seem to be in order between the differing contexts of Jesus' ministry and Paul's. Jesus taught within the context of Israel with its Hebrew assumptions and beliefs. By definition, all Jews were members of the Covenant. Thus any Jew could be seen by any other Jew as a fellow "believer" and heir of God's Covenant. This is not the case with Paul's world. He taught both within and without the boundaries of Judaism, both religiously and geographically. In this new world, neighbors are not necessarily believers. And for Paul as well as for the Apostolic community, only believers are brothers and sisters and fellow recipients of the New Covenant. Any responsible discussion of Christian social ethics needs to incorporate this new and added dimension.[17]

It should therefore come as no big surprise that Paul and the Apostolic community as represented in the book of Acts have no concept of any missionary calling to attempt to impact social structures in any political sense. The *ekklesia* was the divine commonwealth in which the rule of God had already begun. The task was to bring unbelievers into this household and under this rule. Evangelism through the proclamation of the "good news" was the effective means of bringing people into faith and thus into "the Kingdom." Evangelism was the order of the day.

George Ladd has written, "It is difficult to find a clear social ethic in Paul."[18] It is equally difficult to find a clear social ethic in the activities and preaching of the apostles as recorded in the book of Acts. The outstanding incident of what could be termed Apostolic social action is found in Acts 6:1-11. It is the familiar story of how discrimination had developed between the widows of the hellenistic Christians and those of the Palestinian Christians in the daily distribution of food and clothing. The story indicates that the Jerusalem church had indeed gathered necessities from its members for a distribution to those who were unable to take care of themselves. But it was for those *of their number*. Paul's collection for the needy in Jerusalem was for the mother church, not for Jerusalem at large.

The simple fact is that from the book of Acts onward there is no such thing as social action, other than evangelization, outside the immediate environs of the church. Even the much-quoted texts found in James which are often adduced as Scriptural exhortation to social action (especially by Liberation Theologians) are seen, upon examination, to refer to discriminatory behavior that takes place within the church by Christian people (James 2:2). Neither James nor Paul nor the rest of the apostles speak to social structures outside of the church. The reason seems clear. It is not through social action that men are convinced of their sin and brought to the awareness of the need for a Savior; it is through the "foolishness" of preaching that God is calling mankind into His kingdom (1 Corinthians 1:21).

There are further reasons for this clear disinterest in social activity outside the structure of the church on the part of the apostles and of Paul. The social activism of the prophets was limited to the nation of Israel where the theonomous assumption existed. The calls of justice for the oppressed make sense where there is a common understanding that rich and poor alike have God, the Creator, as their common source. Their dignity is derived from a common origin and a divine concern. There is no evidence that the prophets took that message of concern for social justice outside the borders of Israel. When they do go outside of Israel's borders, as in the case of Jonah, it is to call for repentance.

Paul and the apostles believed the church to be an extension of Israel: indeed, even the true Israel (Romans 2:28-29), in which the yoke of the Torah had been replaced with the yoke of Christ (Romans 8:1-4). Thus does James begin his epistle to Christians by addressing them as "the twelve tribes scattered among the nations" (James 1:1). The book of Revelation describes the new Jerusalem as being surrounded by a wall that has twelve foundations upon which appear the names of the "twelve apostles of the Lamb" (Revelation 21:10-14). Since the prophets had limited their social concern to the nation of Israel, and since the apostles and Paul considered the church made of believers in Christ to be the true Israel, it is not surprising that they saw the arena of social activity to be limited to the church. When going outside its border, the prophetic model of Jonah prevailed.

This does not mean that Christians are not to have a social consciousness. It does mean that social activism is not the primary prerequisite for being a Christian. Repentance and faith in Christ are the biblical prerequisites. All else flow from these.

A Final Note

One final point concerning Pauline theology ought to be noted before passing on, and that is Paul's perception of the kingdom as primarily a spiritual rather than a temporal entity. While the church is the temporal center of God's saving activity, the kingdom toward which all this is moving is essentially spiritual and eternal. Thus for Paul, because flesh and blood will not inherit the kingdom (1 Corinthians 15:15), it can never be conceived in materialistic terms such as food and drink, "but of righteousness, peace and joy in the Holy Spirit, because anyone who serves Christ in this way is pleasing to God and approved by men" (Romans 14:17-18).

This is in line with Jesus' teaching about the impropriety

of excessive anxiety about materialism, and the propriety of considerable concern about spirituality that leads beyond this life (with its boundaries of birth and death) to life that is never ending—the final, eternal reality of the kingdom.

As the writer of Hebrews puts it, "People who say such things show that they are looking for a country of their own . . . a heavenly one. Therefore God is not ashamed to be called their God, for he has prepared a city for them" (Hebrews 11:14,16).[19]

Notes

1. C. H. Dodd, *The Apostolic Preaching* (Cleveland: The World Publishing Company, 1957), 11.

2. F. F. Bruce, *New Testament History* (New York: Doubleday and Company, 1969), 208-209. See also Jean Danielou and Henri Marrou, *The Christian Centuries* (London: Paulist Press, 4th edition, 1984), 5-6.

3. Ernst Käseman, *Perspectives on Paul* (Philadelphia: Fortress Press, 1971), 122.

4. The phrase, "at the beginning" makes it quite plain that the apostles saw the day of Pentecost as marking the beginning of the New Covenant or New Age for themselves as believers and for the church. Paul's determination to be at Jerusalem for Pentecost rather than for Passover or Easter illustrates just how important Pentecost was in the minds of the apostolic community (Acts 20:16).

5. Minutes of the Conference of 1774. In his sermon, "Fulness of Faith," Wesley makes clear that he is not making the erroneous distinction of Christians and "Spirit-filled" Christians. He says that not until Pentecost had the disciples received "the end of their faith, even the salvation of their souls," in the New Testament sense.

6. F. F. Bruce, *The Canon of Scripture* (Downers Grove, Ill.: InterVarsity Press, 1988), 28.

7. C. H. Dodd, *The Parables of the Kingdom* (Cleveland: The World Publishing Company, 1957), 77.

8. Ibid., footnotes.

9. This meeting was probably identical with the Jerusalem Council of Acts 15 [J. I. Packer, M.C. Tenney, William White, Jr., eds. *The Bible Almanac* (Nashville: Thomas Nelson Publishers, 1980), 395]. The Jerusalem Council is dated A.D. 49. (See Danielou and Marrou, *The Christian Centuries*, Vol. I, 29-31.)

10. Packer, Tenney, White, eds. *The Bible Almanac*, 599. First Thessalonians is dated A.D. 51-52; 1 Corinthians, A.D. 54; and Galatians, A.D. 55

11. Joseph A. Fitzmeyer, *Pauline Theology* (New York: Prentice-Hall, 1967), 18.

12. The Gospel of Mark was written at about the same time as 1 Thessalonians. Mark is little more than an expanded outline of Apostolic preaching as found in the *kerygma* or earliest proclamations of the good news. C. H. Dodd argues that the terms *gospel* and *kerygma* are identical in actual meaning (*The Apostolic Preaching*, 46-47).

13. Henry Bettenson, ed., *Documents of the Christian Church*, 2nd ed.

(London: Oxford University Press, 1963), 37.

14. One might say that the resurrection of Christ is the most impor- *Also to*
tant doctrine of Christianity. Certainly this was the stumbling block *world*.
between Christians and Jews as represented by the encounters of Acts. *Acts 17!*
But the resurrection of Jesus is not a doctrine, it is an event. The doctrine of justification flows from the event (Romans 4:25).

15. Sanders, *Paul and Palestinian Judaism*, 97.

16. Enslin, *The Ethics of Paul*, Introduction, xii.

17. I would like to suggest at this point that the much disputed interpretation of who are Christ's brothers in the parable of the sheep and
the goats (Matthew 25) has already been spoken to earlier in Matthew
(12:46-50) by our Lord Himself. They are those who do the will of the
heavenly Father which according to John is "to believe on him who he
[the heavenly Father] hath sent" (John 6:29).

18. George Ladd, *A Theology of the New Testament*, 527.

19. For a more complete study of Pauline theology, consult F. F.
Bruce, *Paul, Apostle of the Heart Set Free* and *Jesus and Paul*; George
Ladd, *A Theology of the New Testament*, 359-568; C. H. Dodd, *The
Apostolic Preaching* and *The Meaning of Paul for Today* (Cleveland: The
World Publishing Company, 1957); J. Gresham Machen, *The Origin of
Paul's Religion* (Grand Rapids, Mich.: William B. Eerdman's Publishing
Company, 1925).

Chapter Six

Early Subversions of Evangelical Christianity

Ye are initiated into the mysteries of the Gospel with Paul, the holy, the martyred, inasmuch as he was 'a chosen vessel;' at whose feet may I be found, and at the feet of the rest of the saints, when I shall attain to Jesus Christ . . .

—St. Ignatius, Letter to the Ephesians

We have previously seen that the term "Evangelical" as it applies to a distinct movement in Christian history originated in the Protestant Reformation. It was applied to Martin Luther and his followers, first by his Catholic opponents, and later by the Anabaptists, as a term of distinction and derision. It was further noted that the term arose because of Luther's stubborn insistence on the Pauline doctrine that justification occurs through faith in Christ's substitutionary atonement—faith apart from any human works or merit.

We have also noted that the orthodox wing of the primitive church for the first three centuries of its existence and on into the fourth century, by and large understood Christianity and Christian doctrine and practice to have found its doctrinal expressions and self-understanding through the theology of the apostle Paul. Neither the Apostolic church nor the post-Apostolic church believed that Paul's writings constituted a separate and independent tradition from those of Jesus, as some moderns have argued. Rather, they represent the revelations of the risen and ascended Christ through the Holy Spirit (John 16:12-15) to the apostle Paul in the New Age, specifically for the churches. The Church Age is the New Age, presided over by Messiah, as had been envisioned by the prophets. It is the Age of the New Covenant.

Paul's theology was seen to represent the apex of Christian theology, given by the risen and ascended Christ through the Spirit for the times of the New Covenant. Thus we find St. Ignatius writing these words: "Let Christ speak in us, even as He did in Paul. Let the Holy Spirit teach us to speak the things of Christ in like manner as he did."[1] The veneration of Paul was so great during that period of church history that one patristics scholar has written, "Observe also that the title 'the Apostle' is used frequently by one writer after another to indicate Paul and no one else."[2]

We must now observe that much of Christian history from Apostolic times until the present has been written in terms of the attack on and defense of, the loss and recovery of, the theology of the little man who with joy had "suffered the loss of all things" for the sake of his beloved Master and Savior, Jesus Christ.

Ebionism

One of the earliest of the subversions of Evangelical Christianity came in the form of Ebionism. Ebionite was the name eventually given to the branch of the Judaizers who were active in opposition to the work and soteriology of Paul. The epistles of Galatians and Colossians especially were written by Paul in an attempt to counteract the destructive work of the Judaizers who followed his footsteps, attempting to persuade believers that they must keep the Law of Moses. Whether their insistence on keeping the Law was for initiation into the New Covenant or for salvation, is still being debated. The Ebionites appear to have been divided on the issue of the virgin birth and divinity of Jesus. Some said that belief in His divinity did not matter; others said that it was a matter of consequence.

There is some question as to the origin of their name.[3] "It was probably at first an honorable name for the Jewish Christians, derived from the Hebrew word *Ebion*, 'poor,' alluding to their practice of voluntary poverty . . ."[4] Later the name was applied to a Judaizing group because the orthodox wing of the church saw that their Christology and soteriology were quite deficient. Thus the term came to mean those of an impoverished theology.[5] It is in this sense that Ignatius refers to them in chapter 6 of his letter to the Christians in Philadelphia. And it is also in this sense that early church historian Eusebius refers to the group.[6]

It is the Ebionites who believed in the virgin birth and resurrection of our Lord who are of particular interest to this study. While believing in the divinity of Jesus, they insisted that the Law of Moses be kept also. For them, Jesus was a Hebrew ethicist and upholder of the Mosaic Law. Irenaeus, one of the early church's most important witnesses, tells us: "Those who are called Ebionites . . . use only the Gospel according to Matthew; they reject the Apostle Paul, calling him an apostate from the law. The prophetic writings they strive to expound with especial exactness . . ."[7] At a later date the great early church historian Eusebius writes of them, "They place equal emphasis on the outward observance of the Law. They held that the epistles of the Apostle ought to be rejected altogether, calling him a renegade from the Law; and using only the 'Gospel of the Hebrews,'[8] they treated the rest with scant respect."[9]

The Importance of Eusebius

A word about the importance of Eusebius to our understanding of Christian history would seem to be in order. Born about A.D. 260 in the city of Caesarea, Eusebius lived to see the torture and martyrdom of Christians. He was twice put in prison as a Christian. The first time he and his Christian teacher, Pamphilus, were imprisoned together. Pamphilus was executed.

A prolific writer, Eusebius had access to the theological library that had been established at Caesarea. Later he would do research in libraries in Antioch and Jerusalem. He was appointed Bishop of Caesarea and was offered the See of Antioch, which he declined. He sat at the right hand of Constantine during the Council of Nicaea. His work is as important to the understanding of early church history and historical theology as the Book of Acts is to understanding the church of the Apostolic era and its spread. He has been called "the father of ecclesiastical history—the first, the only historian of the Church bordering on primitive times."[10]

Thus, Eusebius' judgment of the Ebionites is of enormous weight. "It is then because of such practices that they have been dubbed with their present name: Ebionites hints at the poverty of their intelligence, for this is the way in which a poor man is referred to by the Hebrews."[11]

The Ebionites and their relationship to early Christianity and the judgment of earliest Christians (Ignatius, Eusebius, etc.) upon them is of considerable importance. Here we have a group who called themselves Christians; who believed in the divinity of our Lord and His Virgin Birth; who believed in the authority of Scripture. Yet they were regarded as heretics. The reason: they did not accept the theology—and especially the soteriology of the apostle Paul—as being normative for Christianity! Of them Eusebius would write, "They held that they must observe every detail of the Law—by faith in Christ alone, and a life built upon that faith, they would never win salvation."

Is the Law Only a Schoolmaster?

We have previously argued that the Sermon on the Mount and the other ethical instructions of the earthly Jesus are not new in any sense of the word. They are simply rabbinic interpolations of material in the Mosaic Law. Thus it was not the Sermon on the Mount (as found in Matthew, "the Gospel of the Hebrews"), nor Jesus' statement that he had not come to destroy the Law but to fulfill it, that the Ebionites had trouble with. It was the apostle Paul's interpretation that the Law was only a "schoolmaster to bring us to Christ," and that justification is solely by faith in Christ's substitutionary death and His resurrection (Romans 10:9-10) and confession thereto, that troubled them. Like the Anabaptists of Luther's time, they saw Jesus, not as the substitutionary Savior, but as an example to be followed.

The struggles of Ignatius, Eusebius, and others of those early centuries to maintain the purity of orthodoxy as found in the Pauline corpus is mute evidence that Luther's struggles with the Roman Catholics and Anabaptists were not the first struggles concerning this vital issue. Once again it must be stated: Assent to biblical authority is not enough to classify one as "Evangelical." One must also, with the early church leaders and with Luther and the Reformers, give primacy to the Pauline understanding of Christ and His work and what is necessary for salvation as the means of interpreting Scripture.

Pelagianism

At about the same time that Eusebius was combating the heresies of Gnosticism and Ebionism, another movement was beginning. It would become known as monasticism. Historians believe Anthony of Egypt was its initiator.[12] Anthony took literally the admonition of Jesus to the Rich Young Ruler, "If thou wilt be perfect, go and sell that thou hast, and give to the poor, and thou shalt have treasure in heaven: and come and follow me" (Matthew 19:21, KJV). He "sold his large estate, and gave the proceeds to the poor, committing his sister, whose guardian he was, to a body of virgins. He strove to detach himself from the world, and to eradicate all human sensibilities and desires."[13] He went off into seclusion in the wilderness where he fasted, prayed incessantly, and refused to bathe, lest he see his body nude. Thus, monasticism was born. Ultimately the monastic movement would provide the theological leadership for what would become Roman Catholicism.

Christianity was in a state of flux during those early years. Orthodoxy had its hands full articulating and defending itself. A study of patristic literature shows that the orthodox wing of the church continued to look to the writings and theology of Paul for their hermeneutical paradigm and their foil against heresy.

Pelagius, along with a disciple named Celestius, came to Rome. Pelagius was highly regarded in Rome by those who were living the monastic life. Owing to the invasion of the Goths, Pelagius and Celestius moved to Carthage where Celestius settled. Pelagius moved on to Palestine. When applying for ordination to the Bishop at Carthage, Celestius set forth the doctrinal positions that he and Pelagius had arrived at. Chief among these was the teaching that the human race was not fallen; only Adam fell as a result of his disobedience. Every infant is born in a state of sinless perfection and can through choice live a perfect and sinless life.[14] After all, Pelagius had argued, God would not command the impossible. Therefore Jesus' command, "You, therefore, must be perfect, as your heavenly Father is perfect" meant what it said. God's integrity would have prevented Jesus from commanding such if it were not possible.[15]

Pelagius recognized that almost all of mankind is sinful, but attributed that to free moral agency rather than to any inherited disposition toward sin. For those who had fallen into evil he preached justification "by faith alone, through baptism, by reason of the work of Christ."[16]

Though Pelagius affirmed the full divinity of Jesus, he believed that the substitutionary atonement and justification by faith were only for those who had failed at perfection. He rejected the Pauline doctrine of the solidarity of the human race with Adam and the Fall. None other than St. Augustine rose to the dispute. Through several reversals by church synods which convened to hear the dispute, Augustine finally prevailed. After first declaring the Pelagian position free from error, Zosimus, Bishop of Rome, finally acknowledged the position to be in error as regards the biblical doctrine of original sin. A letter was issued in condemnation of the Pelagian position and Pelagius ceased to be of significant theological influence.[17]

The Rise of Roman Catholicism

Though the Pelagian denial of original sin ceased to be of consequence in Western theology, monasticism—with its emphasis on following the ethical teachings of the earthly Jesus in an attempt to reach perfection, to the neglect of Pauline soteriology—continued to grow in influence. Out of the movement eventually rose Roman Catholic soteriology with its view of salvation, partly by faith but very much also by works of supererogation: One must merit the merit of Christ's atoning death.

In behalf of the soteriology of the Catholicism which developed, it must be said that at least it was (and is) logically consistent. This viewpoint came about as a result of certain individuals in the Christian community deciding that the way to salvation was nothing less than getting rid of all earthly goods and following this pathway of worldly renunciation on to perfection (Matthew 19:21). The monastic communities that sprang up had in fact given up *all* earthly possessions and intercourse with the world itself by cloistering themselves away from everyday life as it was lived by ordinary people.

As this soteriological viewpoint became dominant in the West, it raised some additional questions. Clearly, only a small percentage of the population could thus give themselves to the search for perfection. What about the ordinary people—the artisans and governors—without which trade and commerce and the everyday necessities of civilization would not go forward?

The answer to these questions came in the form of a developing spiritual hierarchy with the anchorite (the solitary monk), and the cenobite (the monk who entered the cloister), being at the top; the ordinary *religious* or cleric being next, and the lay person last. Alongside this spiritual hierarchy, an ecclesiastical hierarchy began to emerge.

Since, on a literal reading of Jesus' instructions to the Rich Young Ruler, one may not be saved and enter the kingdom apart from perfection in this life, the search for perfection by the religious orders was indeed intense. No one who was not enrolled in a religious order had a chance to succeed. If one attained to such perfection in this life, they were eventually awarded the title, "saint."

The Doctrine of Purgatory

For the ordinary person as well as for the *religious* who hadn't achieved perfection, Roman Catholic casuistry began to be worked out. And here the doctrine of Purgatory began to surface.

Those who had been baptized and had taken communion were "Christians," but in a state of imperfection. Death therefore might not eternally separate them from heaven. An intermediate state for the purging away of mortal sins would be granted by a loving God.[18] Time in an anticipated Purgatory might be shortened by the giving of alms and the doing of good deeds and acts of penance. It might also be shortened by the prayers and deeds of friends and loved ones who remained in life. The perceived result of one's allotted time in Purgatory was a purification that would ultimately allow entrance into heaven.

Thus did the Apostolic doctrine of justification solely by faith apart from any human works or merit become subverted into the Roman Catholic doctrine of faith plus works of supererogation. Toward the end of the fourth century, voices were raised, warning of the drift away from Apostolic soteriology. The most influential of these was a cleric named Jovinian who, having lived according to the monastic lifestyle, saw its incongruities with Pauline teaching. He went to Rome where he wrote several books on the question, but to no avail.[19]

Thus the *Evangelical* and *Apostolic* faith of those first few centuries was gradually put into a deep sleep. Some centuries later it would be fully awakened by the sound of a hammer, nailing the ninety-five theses to the door of the church at Wittenberg.

Notes

1. Ignatius, *Letter to the Ephesians*. Ignatius lived from A.D. 30-107. A reliable tradition tells us that he, with Polycarp, had been disciples of John. He succeeded Peter as the bishop of Antioch. He was martyred in the Roman arena.

2. Eusebius, *The History of the Church: From Christ to Constantine*, Introduction, 11.

3. While the question of the origin of the Ebionites has not been entirely settled, there is no question that their affinity for the Mosaic Law and their repudiation of Paul certainly links them ideologically with the Judaizers of the first century who caused the Gentile mission so much trouble. Most scholars believe they were in fact the Jerusalem Judaizers who fled the city in A.D. 70 and set up an enclave at Pella.

4. Pakenham-Walsh, *Lights and Shadows of Christendom* (London: Oxford University Press), 11.

5. Ibid., 10-12.

6. Eusebius, *The History of the Church: From Christ to Constantine*, 136-137.

7. Bettenson, ed., *Documents of the Christian Church*, Section on Irenaeus.

8. Irenaeus identifies that which the Ebionites called the "Gospel of the Hebrews" as being the Gospel of Matthew. With its heavy emphasis on the earthly Jesus as the teacher and upholder of the Mosaic Law (which is the real thrust of the Sermon on the Mount), it is no wonder that the Judaizers saw in Matthew, when separated from Paul, justification for their position that the earthly Jesus was primarily a Hebrew ethicist.

9. Eusebius, *The History of the Church: From Christ to Constantine*, 137.

10. Ibid., 7-29.

11. Ibid., 137.

12. Williston Walker, *A History of the Christian Church*, rev. ed. (New York: Charles Scribner's Sons, 1959), 125.

13. Albert H. Newman, *A Manual of Church History*, Vol. I (Chicago: The American Baptist Publication Society, 1931), 317.

14. The position of Pelagius is exactly the same as the rabbinical position. Augustine countered the faulty anthropology of Pelagius with Paul's doctrine of the solidarity of the human race with the fall of Adam. Paul's position was not necessarily that of the rabbis on all issues.

15. W. H. C. Frend, *The Rise of Christianity* (Philadelphia: Fortress

Press, 1984), 674; Parkenham-Walsh, *Lights and Shadows of Christendom*, 206.

16. Walker, *A History of the Christian Church*, 168.

17. Ibid., 169-170.

18. Martin Jugie, *Purgatory and the Means to Avoid It* (The Newman Press, Westminster, Maryland, 1949; translated from the seventh French ed. by Malachy Gerard Carroll).

19. A. C. McGiffert, *A History of Christian Thought*, Vol. II, *The West from Tertullian to Erasmus* (Scribner's: New York, 1950), 62-68.

Chapter Seven

Evangelicalism and Hermeneutics

The sound of Luther's hammer, echoing through the streets of Wittenberg, signaled the return of the Apostolic hermeneutic to center stage in biblical studies and interpretation. The two cornerstones upon which the Reformation rests are the final authority of the Scriptures in matters of faith and practice and that justification is solely by faith apart from human works of merit.

It is now time to point out that the doctrine of justification by faith was seen by the Reformers and by John Wesley to be the hermeneutical paradigm by which the Scriptures are to be interpreted. In order to do that, we must return briefly to that moment in church history that has become known as Luther's "tower discovery." This "tower discovery" would in turn translate itself into what may be termed Wesley's "Aldersgate discovery"—a discovery that would trigger the great Evangelical revival in England and which, in turn, would become the fountainhead of the modern Evangelical movement.

Because of the well known and well documented "traditions" of the Roman Catholic Church which were given equal and sometimes even superior authority to the Scriptures, Protestants have often supposed that Luther's problem was caused primarily by the Catholic use of these traditions to interpret Scripture. But a careful study of Luther's life and struggles will not support this conclusion. His initial problem was not caused by Catholic casuistry and tradition. His problem was, How do you interpret authoritative Scripture? And his special problem was, *how does one interpret the Sermon on the Mount in the light of human frailty?* Only after he had solved that crucial question did Roman Catholic tradition become a problem for Luther. The reasons for this will presently become clear.

Luther and Biblical Interpretation

Once again let us point out that the Roman Catholic Church of Luther's time taught that justification came only at the end of a long process. Baptism, confirmation, communion, penance, and works of supererogation or merit—all these were signs that one had embarked upon the road to justification. But to declare the sinner justified indicated that the sinner was also declared to be righteous or in right standing with God. According to established Catholic soteriology, one could not be declared "justified" until one had become *perfect*. And this, according to established Catholic doctrine, could not possibly take place until sufficient works of penance and supererogation had finally done their work of "perfecting." Therein lay Luther's problem.

It was clear to Luther (and also to John Wesley[1])—even if it does not seem clear to many modern interpreters—that the bottom line of the Sermon on the Mount was Jesus' instruction to the disciples that they must be perfect as God was perfect, if they would enter the kingdom (Matthew 5:48). This of course, went hand in glove with Catholic soteriology. One must become perfect through renouncing worldly ambition, worldly goods, fleshly desires, even marriage; and embark on a road of service and self-mortification. Only at the end of this process could one hope in this life to be so perfected, and thus be declared by a righteous God to be "justified." The elite few who accomplish this could go straight in to the Eternal Presence at death. For the rest, the fires of Purgatory waited.

Having done all that the Catholic Church had prescribed, Luther realized that instead of coming closer to the perfection demanded in the Sermon on the Mount, he was, if anything, farther from home. Thus Todd observes that the cause of Luther's depression and anguish of spirit was "despair at the impossibility of success in the task which the Christian apparently faced, the task of being good enough for God, the complete impossibility of a total purity of motive and of total perfection such as Jesus commands in the Sermon on the Mount."[2]

The point of this is that when any group—Catholic or otherwise, regardless of what banner they choose to march under—switches the primary emphasis of Scripture from the Pauline doctrine of justification as a gracious gift from

Christ conditioned only by faith, to justification as a reward for following the earthly teachings of our Lord (no matter how faithfully), *the honest person is compelled to despair.*

It is just here that we need to pay strict attention to the hermeneutical question, especially as addressed by Luther and Wesley. Yes, Scripture is the final authority in all matters of faith and practice. But it is Scripture *informed and interpreted by the doctrine of justification solely by faith in God's forgiving grace,* manifested and made possible by Christ's substitutionary atonement.

This doctrine was affirmed at the Jerusalem Council (Acts 15) as being central to the Apostolic understanding of the essence of Christian soteriology. It finds its clearest and most complete articulation in the writings of Paul to the young churches under his care. This most important of biblical doctrines came to a single brilliant beam of focused light for Luther in Romans 1:17: "The just shall live by faith."

Later, reflecting on his discovery of the meaning of this verse as the biblical pathway to salvation, Luther wrote, "This immediately made me feel as if I was reborn, and as though I had entered through open gates into paradise itself. From then on, *the whole face of Scripture* [italics mine] appeared different."[3] In discovering the key to correct biblical interpretation, Luther discovered also "the keys to the kingdom"!

Some years later, through his *Preface to Romans,* he would pass these keys on to a struggling and depressed Anglican Churchman named John Wesley, who as a result would begin lighting the fires of "evangelicalism" in England; fires that would spread to America and the New

World. Wesley too had found the answer to consistent biblical interpretation through the Pauline doctrine of justification solely by faith. From then on for Wesley also, the whole face of Scripture appeared different. "And I saw more than ever that the gospel is in truth but one great promise from beginning to end."

It was this soteriological and hermeneutical insight that caused Wesley to become, in his own words, "a man of one book"—the Bible. The doctrine of justification by faith became the lens that brought into focus the Scriptures in their entirety. While tradition, reason, and experience, would also play important roles in Wesley's scheme of religious authority, after Aldersgate none of them were allowed to assume a position of ascendancy over the primacy of Scriptural authority.

What Place the Sermon on the Mount?

How then did Luther and Wesley come to regard the Sermon on the Mount? Both men, being the astute students of the Scriptures that they were, came to the very conclusion that informed modern scholarship, both Jewish and Christian, is coming to. They judged that the Sermon on the Mount represents Jesus at His "prophetic" best—as an upholder of the Mosaic Law in its every detail. Both, taking their cue from Paul in Romans 7, saw the Law, of which the Sermon on the Mount is a summation, as functioning in the role of condemnation, *not* salvation. The stern precepts of the Sermon on the Mount are to be preached, not as a torturous pathway to salvation, as in Monasticism, nor as a teaching around which to form a semi-ascetic community, as in Anabaptism. *The Sermon is to be preached in all of its rigors to destroy any hopes of self-righteousness.*

This in turn has the effect described by Paul of causing the sinner to see his situation of utter helplessness and to cry out, "O wretched man that I am; who shall deliver me from the body of this death" (Romans 7:24)? Human pride and confidence having now been destroyed by the Sermon on the Mount (which is but a summation of the Mosaic Law), the penitent is in position to receive the gospel, the "good news:" "I thank God through Jesus Christ" (Romans 7:25).

Thus Wesley writes, "By 'preaching the law' I mean explaining and enforcing the commands of Christ briefly comprised in the Sermon on the Mount. I mean by 'preaching the Gospel,' preaching the love of God to sinners, preaching the life, death, resurrection and intercession of Christ, with all the blessings which in consequence thereof are freely given to true believers."[4]

This is nothing but Evangelicalism!

We must conclude therefore that Pauline theology and soteriology constitute the original Apostolic Tradition as witnessed to by the Jerusalem Conference of Acts 15, as well as the early, orthodox Patristic writings. The rise of the Monastic movement encouraged interpreters to use the teachings of the earthly Jesus as the primary hermeneutical grid. This in turn resulted in the gradual loss of the Apostolic soteriological and hermeneutical tradition, which would one day be recovered by Luther and the Reformers and become known as Evangelicalism.

We can only deduce that the Apostolic Tradition and orthodox Evangelicalism are ONE!

Notes

1. See Wesley's letter of response dated London, December 20, 1751.
2. John M. Todd, *Martin Luther* (New York: The Paulist Press, 1964), 35.
3. Ibid., 78.
4. Letter, December 20, 1751.

Chapter Eight

The Rise of the New Evangelical Left

With these things in mind, students of the contemporary Evangelical scene must look with some misgivings at a clearly discernable trend in some quarters of the Evangelical movement: the trend to belittle or even ignore Paul's historic role as the church's primary interpreter. Voices are being raised that are calling for a "balanced" view of Scripture. The clear implication is that the traditional Evangelical way of doing theology and Christian ethics is "unbalanced." As one further reads some of the material coming from the new Evangelical left, it becomes clear that the traditional Evangelical reliance on Paul is perceived as a regrettable error!

Thus we find self-styled "young Evangelical" Richard Quebedeaux suggesting that the proclivity of Evangelicalism to depend on Paul to interpret Scripture is the result of the Dispensationalism of J. N. Darby and C. I. Scofield. He goes on to suggest that the affinity for Paul is why "Fundamentalist and Evangelical pulpits" do not stress the social message of the prophets and the ethical teaching of Jesus.

Inasmuch as Quebedeaux is considered one of the intellectual leaders of the new "Evangelical" left, perhaps it will be permissible to stick to these points by way of answer and critique on the movement generally.[1]

The Ancient Priority of Paul

In the first place, the turning to Paul as a means of interpreting Scripture did not historically originate with the Dispensational method of viewing Scripture. It originated in Apostolic times and was rediscovered during the Reformation by Luther and the Reformers, and later by John Wesley. That there was a hermeneutical shift in and around the time of the completion of the canon (A.D. 393)[2] has previously been acknowledged in this study. But we must recall that this shift was away from Paul who had been the primary theologian of both the Apostolic and Patristic eras.[3] It must be further noted that this was the hermeneutical shift that ultimately gave rise to Roman Catholic soteriology and casuistry, a point that Quebedeaux seems not to appreciate.

In addition, the epistles of Paul were the first Christian writings to be considered authoritative Scripture by the Apostolic community. Later the Gospels would join the writings of Paul in being regarded as having the same "inspired" status as did the writings of the Old Testament. The Pauline corpus, with the four Gospels, were the first writings by Christians to be regarded as authoritative, with Paul's writings having the undisputed distinction of being the first such writings so regarded. It was this group of writings that *all other writings* were measured against for theological content. And thus the concept of "canon" or "measuring stick" was born. If one objects to the idea of "a canon within the canon" therefore, the objection must be lodged on grounds other than the historical facts.[4]

If referring to the dearth of preaching the social message of the prophets and the ethical teachings of Jesus, Quebedeaux raises another interesting hermeneutical question. The social message of the prophets was not some new and special revelation that came *ex nihilo* from Yahweh. The prophets were the true religious conservatives of Israel. The Torah was the cornerstone of the religion of Yahweh. It was the social provisions in the Mosaic Law that were being violated by the nation of Israel. The prophetic polemic against certain abuses in the nation, whether the subject was Sabbath breaking or the oppression of the poor, had its origins and its authority in the Mosaic Law. It was disregard for the various provisions of the Torah that evoked the prophetic response.

Now as Paul (a Hebrew of Hebrews) perceived, the Mosaic Law stands or falls as a whole. Many would-be interpreters of the Old Testament seem to thrive on picking texts that fit a presupposed agenda. Correct hermeneutics will acknowledge that if the proscriptions are authoritative for all time in one text—such as the provisions for cancelling loans every seven years (Deuteronomy 15:1-11)—the proscriptions are authoritative for all time also for such texts as those that enforce the rite of circumcision. This hermeneutical smorgasbord mentality is sharply criticized by Harvard scholar G. F. Moore: "It is obvious . . . that the scripture gives no warrant whatever for dividing the law into ceremonial and moral . . . It is not for man to cavil about its prescription of interdictions, or to exempt himself from any of them."[5]

Was it not this very tendency among the Pharisees that brought about Jesus' caustic comment, "Woe to you, teachers of the law and Pharisees, you hypocrites! You give a tenth of your spices—mint, dill and cumin. But you have neglected the more important matters of the law—justice, mercy and faithfulness. You should have practiced the latter, *without neglecting the former*" (Matthew 23:23, italics mine).[6] Jesus well knew that the Mosaic Law stands or falls as a unit (Matthew 5:17,18).

In Christianity we recognize that we have been freed from the necessity of the rite of circumcision, Sabbatarian regulations, and a host of other provisions found in the Mosaic Law. If we had only the teachings of the earthly Jesus on this matter, we would still be bound to keep all of these as well as the whole body of Mosaic teachings, right down to every jot and tittle. Ponder for a moment a New Testament that ends with the Gospel of John!

Free from the Law

The freedoms we enjoy in the Christian faith do not emanate from the *teachings* of the earthly Jesus who came to the nation of Israel as a prophet and rabbi and upholder of the Law. Christian liberty and Christian ethics come from the instructions of the risen and ascended Christ through His apostles in the new and final age—the age of the Church.

Sharp distinctions exist between the Old Covenant, which was based on the animal sacrificial system and the Torah, and the New Covenant, based on the once-and-for-all sacrifice of the spotless lamb of God and grounded in much better promises. In his sermon on Christian Perfection, Wesley wrote, "It is of great importance to observe, and that more carefully than is commonly done, the wide difference there is between the Jewish and the Christian dispensation. . . ." The writer of Hebrews observes that the Old Covenant contained "a mere shadow of things to come" (Hebrews 10:1).

James 2:19 is often quoted to refute the doctrine of justification by faith alone. Several things need to be said here. First, any interpretation that sets James against Paul is clearly unneccessary. James is not rejecting faith, but rather is trying to describe its nature. He begins his discussion by writing, "What good is it, my brothers, if a man *claims to have faith* but has no deeds?" (James 2:14, italics mine). He has no intention of setting aside faith; much to the contrary, he is attempting to clarify what it is and what it does. That is why he then says, "Show me your faith without deeds, *and I will show you my faith by what I do* (James 2:18, italics mine). There is no necessary contradiction between Paul and James.

Second, although James was known from a rather early period in Christian history, it was not included in the canon of Scripture until the Council of Hippo in A.D. 393. This certainly says something about the weight of the epistle in the eyes of the earliest church, especially in view of the fact that Paul's letters were *never* held at arm's length or questioned, and in fact were the first Christian writings (both chronologically and actually) to be accepted as Scripture.

Since the earliest church got along quite well for nearly three hundred years without the authoritative use of this document, and since the interpretation of the verse in question is somewhat unclear, it would seem the height of proof-texting at its most questionable to so cavalierly use this verse to overthrow one of the key doctrines of the New Covenant. Thus F. F. Bruce notes that "in the evangelical tradition generally, the four chief Pauline epistles (Romans, 1 and 2 Corinthians, Galatians) play a leading part in the effective canon . . ."!

Was Jesus a Revolutionary?

Finally, there is an influential group of thinkers in our time, part of whom identify themselves as "Evangelicals," who would have us believe that Jesus was a religious and political revolutionary who was finally crucified for His "prophetic" and "revolutionary" activity in behalf of the poor. The earthly Jesus is pictured by this group as the model for Christian political involvement in subversive causes.

Such interpreters overlook some important information.

First, they often refer to Jesus' famous sermon in Luke 4:14-27 as a summons to political activism in behalf of the economically poor and oppressed of the world. But if this be true, the main thrust of the message was somehow lost on the disciples. There is no evidence that they engaged in any such activity, save in behalf of their own poor (Acts 6:1-6). This does not mean that Christians should be uninvolved in humanitarian concerns; it does mean that such concerns must be established in some other way.

At Jesus' trial, the Jewish Sanhedrin could not find one

offense or breach of the Mosaic Law, reminding us of Jesus' previously unanswered challenge, "Can any of you prove me guilty of sin" (John 8:46)? In the end, the only charge they could bring was that of blasphemy for having said that He was "the son of God," the Messiah.[7] But of course, this is the affirmation that formed the watershed between those who became known as Christians and those who remained unbelieving. It remains so to the present hour.

Jesus was tried on that awful night by both Pilate and Herod Antipas to see if any charges of political subversive activity against Rome and Roman rule might be brought. In the end, Herod Antipas, who was so fearful of the possibility of political competitors that he had committed murder and infanticide, sent Jesus back to Pilate with no sentence of condemnation. He saw only a disillusioned rabbi who had been rejected by His own nation. Pilate's own judgment on Jesus as a possible political subversive has come down to us in these words: "I find in him no fault" (John 18:38).

A Final Observation

In view of these things, a final observation seems in order. The responsible biblical interpreter must always beware of allowing personal, cherished presuppositions about the nature of history and reality to become a filter through which to do biblical hermeneutics. One of the key distinctions between the historic Christian faith and the religions that surrounded it was the assumption of the totally voluntary self-disclosure of God—the primary reality of all that exists.

Commenting on this very point, Emil Brunner has observed, "The Christian understanding of reality is of a very different kind (from other religions). . . . It is determined by the thought that God is the creator and the world is His creation. God therefore is the primary reality. Whatever else we call real is secondary, dependent reality."[8] The self-revealed, transcendent God of the Bible no more speaks with a Hebrew accent than with a German or Hispanic accent.

This means, of course, that any time a theologian or would-be theologian uses humanity and the human or cultural experience as the primary starting point, whatever else they are up to, they are not doing biblical theology. Any time we sacralize anything other than the personal, transcendent God of the Bible, we are guilty of committing the sin of idolatry. And any starting point for "doing theology" that has an assumption other than the basic assumption of Genesis 1, is bound to result in theological aberration and even heresy.

Nor is the essence of Evangelicalism to be found in some subjective religious experience, regardless of how cherished. Religious experience is, after all, the common denominator of all religions.[9]

The essence of Evangelicalism is to be found in how one interprets an authoritative Bible in light of the doctrine of justification solely by faith. Experience serves only to confirm what the Scriptures, illumined by the light of this greatest of Evangelical doctrines, has made clear.

Notes

1. Richard Quebedeaux, *The Young Evangelicals*, 76-81.

2. F. F. Bruce, *The Books and the Parchments* (Westwood, N.J.: Fleming H. Revell Company, 1950), 113.

3. Williston Walker, *A History of the Christian Church*, rev. ed. (New York: Charles Scribner's Sons, 1959), 125-128; W. H. C. Frend, *The Rise of Christianity* (Philadelphia: Fortress Press, 1984), 54.

4. Bruce, *The Books and the Parchments*, 104-113.

5. G. F. Moore, *Judaism*, Vol. II, 6-7.

6. See also Emil Brunner, *Justice and the Social Order* (Harper Brothers, 1945), 118-120.

7. F. F. Bruce, *New Testament History* (New York: Doubleday and Company, 1969), 197.

8. Emil Brunner, *Christianity and Civilization* (London, Nisbit & Co., Ltd., 1948), 17-18.

9. For an excellent discussion of this point see William James' classic, *The Varieties of Religious Experience*.

Chapter Nine

Needed:
A New
Reformation

Morton Scott Enslin has written, "In all reverence it may be said that had it not been for Paul or someone like him, there is good reason to believe there never would have been any Christianity."[1]

The death and resurrection of Jesus and the descent of the Holy Spirit at Pentecost, while bringing an entirely new understanding to the disciples about who Jesus had really been and what salvation consisted of, still left them with a considerable hermeneutical problem. They now knew that acceptance of Jesus as the Anointed One of God constituted the heart of the gospel (Acts 2:14-36). The calling of Peter to the household of the Roman centurion

Cornelius and the gift of salvation through their response of faith without the trappings of the Mosaic Law raised an additional problem. What then had been the purpose of the Law? And how should the Christian community interpret the Scriptures of the Old Testament which were understood to be the basis of the overall tradition?

How Do We Interpret Scripture?

We must note once again that many of the teachings of the earthly Jesus had, if anything, strengthened the authority of the Mosaic Law. Thus it is not at all surprising to find Jewish Pharisees who counted themselves as Christians because they accepted the resurrection of Jesus, but who insisted that Christianity consisted not of simple faith in Christ's atonement but also in following the Mosaic Law (Acts 15:5). After all, had not Jesus Himself taught in the Sermon on the Mount that He had not come to destroy the Law, but to fulfill it (Matthew 5:17-20)?

They all believed in biblical authority. Now the question that pressed itself upon them was, "How shall the Christian community read and interpret the Scriptures?" This was a particularly difficult question, for the earthly Jesus had not addressed it in such a way that the new understanding of the meaning of salvation could be established by the only Scriptures they then were in possession of—namely, the Scriptures of the Old Testament.

In his book, *Perspectives on Paul*, Ernst Käseman notes that this critical hermeneutical problem was solved by the apostle Paul. Jesus had told the disciples that they would not fully comprehend all that He had been about until the descent of the Spirit (John 16:7-15). Peter began the preaching of justification by faith (Acts 10:43), but it was

Paul who gave it a biblical foundation by appealing to the justification of Abraham by faith before the Law was ever in place (Romans 4; Galatians 3). Thus Käseman writes, "For the first time the problem of a Christian hermeneutic became a theological theme."[2]

The importance of this observation can scarcely be over-estimated. Without Paul's inspired use of Abraham's justification by faith before the entry of the Mosaic Law, a Christian interpretation of the meaning of salvation solely through faith lacked sufficient scriptural base. Now a firm biblical basis for the doctrine had been established and a Christian hermeneutic began to emerge as a clear cut option to the biblical hermeneutic of the Judaizers. The isolation of "faith" as the effective cause of Abraham's justification—rather than merit as in rabbinical Judaism—opened the door to the possibility of the member of any race or sex becoming a "true Israelite."

But this is not all that Käseman observes about the importance of Paul to Christian theology. He says, "In the whole of the New Testament it is only Paul who expounds what we should call a thoroughly thought-out doctrine of man . . ."[3] He goes on to observe that the centerpiece of Paul's soteriology begins with the solidarity of the human race in the fall of Adam and the solidarity of believers with Christ in salvation through faith. Since our salvation has been wrought by Christ Jesus through his cross, and not through anything we have done, and since this salvation has been made available in the New Age and under the New Covenant, "redemption is to be understood as eschatological *creatio ex nihilo*."[4] Or to put it in Paul's words, "Not by works of righteousness which we have done, but according to his mercy he saved us" (Titus 3:5, KJV).

Käseman's observation points up two things: first, the importance of the hermeneutical question; and second, the absolute importance of the place of Paul as the articulator of Christian theology.

It has been previously noted that there is general agreement that the two salient features of Evangelicalism are assent to biblical authority on questions of faith and practice, and the doctrine of justification by faith. We must now note that the doctrine of justification *solely by faith* (in the forensic sense[5]) has its origin in Paul's soteriology. The use of Abraham as a biblical model for justification by faith first appeared in writing in Paul's letter to the Galatians (Galatians 3)[6] at the height of the Judaizing controversy and set the tone for the discussion of the nature of salvation from that time onward.

It must therefore be insisted that assent to biblical authority is only a first step in doing Evangelical theology. The next step is to acknowledge with the early church, the Continental Reformers, the English Baptists, and John Wesley, that *the theology of Paul is the hermeneutical paradigm by and through which Scripture and the Christ event are to be interpreted.*

Pauline theology and Apostolic Tradition historically go hand in hand. Thus the battle for Paul in our day is nothing more nor less than a battle for historic Christianity. If Evangelicalism is to recover its effectiveness and vitality, it must once again assert the theology of Paul as its hermeneutical paradigm.

Features of an Evangelical Theology

The following are the salient features of an Evangelicalism based on Pauline theology:

1. The doctrine of justification solely by faith, apart from any human merit or works;

2. The doctrine of original sin and the solidarity of the entire human race in Adam's Fall;

3. The priority of evangelism over social action;

4. The continuing recognition of the imminence (not immediacy) of the parousia.

Inevitably the Pauline hermeneutic will include such things as Paul's judgment concerning the sinfulness and unacceptability of homosexual practice and his judgment concerning the respective roles of husbands, wives, and children in the Christian household. A refined Evangelicalism will take its stand on these issues because they proceed from the authority of the risen and ascended Lord through His "chosen vessel" for the church.

The Doctrine of Justification Solely by Faith

There are not two doctrines of salvation in the New Testament, one by faith and one by works. Correct hermeneutics allow for only one avenue of salvation: solely through faith, solely by God's grace. The basis of Christian fellowship in the Church Universal lies in the acknowledgment that we all come into the kingdom as beggars. The robe of righteousness we wear has been woven on the loom of God's eternal grace; it has been purchased for each and all by our Lord, Jesus Christ.

There are not two gospels, one of Jesus and one of Paul. As the "chosen vessel" of the risen and ascended Christ, Paul was chosen to define and interpret the full meaning of the coming of our Lord. Thus C. H. Dodd correctly observes that when we learn from Paul, "we shall have learned what Christianity is, from the man who though he knew not Christ after the flesh, divined better than any what Christ stood and stands for."[7] Clearly, the post-Pentecostal Apostolic understandings of the meaning of the "gospel" and Pauline understandings are one.

The Doctrine of Original Sin

Unique to Pauline insight is the teaching, given under inspiration of the Holy Spirit, that *all mankind* is involved in the Fall of Adam. This statement always has and always will clash with the proud and sinful heart and mind of autonomous man. It is this proclamation that drives one to either accept the substitutionary salvation of Jesus Christ in helpless humility, or create "another gospel." It is this understanding of the eternal lostness of man that fuels the missionary enterprise.

It was precisely at this point that the Judaizers were faulted by Paul. The rabbis had taught that while man sins, man is not essentially and necessarily sinful. In rabbinical anthropology, man is not fallen and therefore does not need a Savior.[8] To this Paul gave a resounding *no!* In Adam, all have died. Only in Christ will all be made alive. Paul's diametrically differing anthropological viewpoint with rabbinical anthropology ought to make us very cautious about superimposing rabbinism and its teachings onto Paul, even though he had been a rabbi.

It is this doctrine that humanists from Erasmus (the father of Continental Anabaptism)[9] to the secular humanists of today need to hear preached. This is the great leveler of rich and poor, learned and unlearned, oppressed and oppressor: all stand under this judgment. It was this doctrine that exposed the Pelagian heresy and caused the teachings of Gnostics and Ebionites alike to be labeled as unorthodox.

If we are born with a fatal flaw, we cannot hope to be perfect as God is perfect without help from outside ourselves. Even the believer continues to be subject to temptation, failure, and sin. The perfect righteousness of Jesus Christ, imputed and imparted through faith, is the only answer to Christ's command, "Be ye therefore perfect, even as your Father which is in heaven is perfect" (Matthew 5:48, KJV). This robe of righteousness, as Zinzendorf observed, is the only clothing that will be able to survive the flames of God's eschatological judgment (see 1 Corinthians 3).

It was the preaching of this doctrine that brought John Wesley such persecution and disbarment from the Anglican pulpits.[10] In the minutes of Wesley's first annual conference, the question was asked, "In what sense is Adam's sin imputed to all mankind?" Wesley's answer: "In Adam all died—i.e. 1) our bodies then became mortal; 2) our souls died—i.e. were disunited from God; 3) and hence we are all born with a sinful devilish nature, by reason whereof 4) we all are children of wrath, liable to death eternal."[11] There is no universal God-mysticism here! It was only when Wesley realized his helplessness to achieve the perfection demanded by Christ in the Sermon on the Mount, through the failure of the Georgia mission, that he was ready to receive the justification that comes by faith alone. Luther and Wesley had had the Sermon on the Mount. They were saved when they encountered the preaching of Paul!

The Priority of Evangelism Over Social Action

If all mankind is lost apart from Jesus Christ, then evangelism must be the order of the day. For Paul, evangelism meant going into the synagogues of the Jews of the Diaspora and into the marketplaces of the Gentiles and there proclaiming "Christ and him crucified, the wisdom of God and the power of God unto salvation, to everyone that believeth." *There is no evidence that Paul saw social activism as being a sign of discipleship.*

Thus George Ladd says of Paul, "He was unconcerned about 'social ethics'—the impact of the gospel on social structures . . . The Christian faith is to be lived out within the context of existing social structures, for they belong to the form of this world, which is passing away (I Cor. 7:31) . . . There is no evidence that Paul looked upon the church as a structure that would take its place with other social structures and change them for the good."[12]

Evangelism and the missionary endeavor was everything to Paul. Many Evangelicals who are social activists point to John Wesley's activism in behalf of the prisoners of war and the orphans of society. But it must be noted that after Aldersgate, Wesley's burning passion was evangelism. He did not cease being socially conscious and involved (nor should we), but there came a great shift in the amount of time and energy he spent on social projects *vis a vis* the time and energy spent on evangelism.

To put it concretely, Wesley did not ride those thousands of weary miles on horseback carrying placards reading, "Better working conditions for miners." He rode them with an open Bible in his hand, preparing to offer justification by faith through God's free grace in another corner of his beloved England. And thus the condition of thousands of miners as well as their families was changed in the only manner that will have ultimate significance. As C. H. Dodd has observed, "It was by *kerygma*, says Paul, not by *didache*, that it pleased God to save men."[13]

The Recognition of the Imminence of the Parousia

There can be no question that Paul's social or horizontal outlook was conditioned by his certainty of the imminence of the *parousia*, the Second Coming of Christ. That this expectation was not immediately fulfilled is no reason for its present abandonment. Our Lord specifically warned about the possible consequences of such a mistake (Matthew 24:45-51; Luke 12:42-46).

The belief in the imminence of the *parousia* (not immediacy), is the tension that keeps things in their proper perspective. It also serves as a constant reminder as to who is the Director of this cosmic drama. The idea that we can, by our efforts and coalitions, bring the kingdom to earth is most gratifying to our prideful, egoistic nature. But the idea that at God's command, Christ may break in at any moment, right when we were about to earn our Ph.D. or bring about world disarmament, is of course somewhat discomfiting. Yet it keeps things in proper focus, for it reminds us that all social structures will pass away.

Even the church must have the wheat separated from the tares before it is ready for God's immediate presence. Thus we believe J. Murray to have been correct when he wrote, "The eschatological perspective should always characterize our attitude to things temporal and temporary.[14]

The Importance of Doctrine

Finally, if Evangelicalism is to recover its vitality, it seems clear that it must recover a renewed interest in the absolute importance of biblical doctrine. Many of the New Evangelical Left decry the necessity of doctrine, even going so far as to suggest that doctrine is relatively unimportant, deeds are all important.[15]

A quick look into the instructions of the apostle Paul to two of the young Christian pastors under his care (Timothy and Titus) ought to dispel any such notion. The urgency with which Paul instructs them to study, to preach, and to teach sound doctrine, is a constant theme of Paul's pastorals.

It should not be forgotten that virtually all of the heresies the Christian church has had to confront from the Apostolic period until now have been dealt with either by Paul at first hand (the Judaizers and Gnostics), or by Paul through his writings (the Pelagian heresy dealt with by Augustine, the Catholic soteriological heresy dealt with by Luther). It is impossible to overestimate the importance of the Pauline hermeneutic in the interpretation of Scripture and in the success or failure of the church, the Evangelical enterprise, and the maintenance of Christian orthodoxy.

The Testimony of John

In this struggle to define, defend, and maintain historic Evangelicalism as articulated by the "chosen vessel," the apostle Paul, there is another important witness who must be heard. He is none other than the beloved disciple John.

John holds a unique place among the eyewitnesses of Jesus. He was probably the youngest of the original Twelve.

He was one of Jesus' inner circle of friends. He leaned on his Master at the Last Supper. He was the only disciple to accompany Jesus into the trial hall of Pilate, just as he was the only disciple to stand by the cross of his Lord in open identification and companionship, even until death. He was the first disciple to believe in the reality of the resurrection (John 20:8). He was the last living eyewitness of the incarnation of our Lord. And finally, his writings constitute the last of the canonical Scriptures to be written. Thus the testimony of John is of enormous importance.

John's Gospel probably was not composed until near the end of the first century. Therefore he commanded a perspective on the history and developments, particularly theological developments, of the gospel and Christian theology which the others did not enjoy.

As we study the Gospel of John, we are struck by the thematic similarity of its contents with the writings of Paul. The emphasis in John is on "belief" (by implication, faith) in Jesus as the means of salvation. From the beginning to the end of his Gospel, the theme of believing in Christ is of utmost soteriological importance. He tells his readers that he has written his Gospel in order that "you may believe that Jesus is the Christ, the Son of God, and that by believing you may have life in his name" (John 20:31).

John refers to believing or belief as the essence of salvation three times more often than the writers of the synoptics taken together. When one recalls Paul's instructions to the terrified Philippian jailer, "Believe on the Lord Jesus Christ and thou shalt be saved" (Acts 16:31, KJV), along with the multitude of times belief in Christ and Christ alone is exalted in his epistles as the key to salvation, one cannot help but conclude that the doctrine of justification by faith, apart from human works or merit, was indeed the understanding held by the Apostolic church as a whole, not just by Paul.

A second important motif in John that parallels Paul's understanding is that of the dualistic nature of existence. While the synoptics continue to view time as moving on a horizontal plane from the Old Age to the New, John juxtaposes the *world above* with the *world below*, with the Christian living in the evil world below physically but having spiritual origin and life in the world above. While there are some minor differences in this viewpoint with Paul, it is essentially the same.[16]

Even as Paul discerns that this Age which continues on its way toward the end is controlled by the rulers and authorities "of this dark world" (Ephesians 6:10-12; Romans 8:38), so John sees this world as ruled by Satanic power and authority (John 16:11). In this regard it is interesting to hear Jesus say to a certain group of Pharisees, "You belong to your father, the devil, and you want to carry out your father's desires" (John 8:44). The Sermon on the Mount does not appear in this last-to-be-written Gospel— a fact of considerable significance in itself!

There are several verses of this Gospel that seem to sum up John's position (i.e., John 3:16). But one that may sum up John's understanding of the essence of the gospel and of salvation appears in the sixth chapter. In answer to the question, "What must we do to work the works God requires?" Jesus answered, "The work of God is this: to believe in the one he has sent" (John 6:28-29). Or as Paul put it, "That if you confess with your mouth the Lord Jesus, and believe in your heart that God has raised him from the dead, you shall be saved" (Romans 10:9, KJV).

Radical Christianity

Back in 1980, Clark Pinnock observed, "I see a watering down of evangelical convictions which appears also in issues like feminism and homosexuality, where the expectations of the circle we move in are very powerful, and make us wish to have the Scriptures agree with them."[17] As one encounters the work of the New Evangelical Left, a distinct impression is given that perhaps they are doing their work more to impress the academicians of the liberal wing of the church and the secular humanists, than to defend and proclaim "the faith that was once for all entrusted to the saints" (Jude 3). Thus Francis Schaeffer observed in 1984:

> Many young evangelicals earned their undergraduate and graduate degrees from the finest secular schools. But something happened in the process. In the midst of totally humanistic colleges and universities, and a totally humanistic orientation in the academic disciplines, many of these young evangelicals began to be infiltrated by the anti-Christian world view which dominated the thinking of their colleges and professors. In the process, any distinctively evangelical Christian point of view was accommodated to the secularistic thinking in their disciplines and to the surrounding world spirit of our age.[18]

"We are still trying to please the committee of secularism," writes Harold Fickett, "grateful just to *pass*."[19]

Certainly, the pressures to conform and to show what are regarded as "signs of intellectual ability" in the mainline seminaries and prestigious universities are enormous. But the truly "radical" Evangelical Christian will consult the Scriptures first and last. If their instruction is contrary to the prevailing assumptions of modernity, whether it be concerning questions raised by militant feminism or questions raised by the gay rights movement, our task is to "speak the truth in love" (Ephesians 4:14-16); not as those who have arrived or already been made perfect, but as those who understand judgment, repentance, and forgiveness through faith in Christ.

Again it is Paul who speaks to the question in this fashion: "Do not conform any longer to the pattern of this world, but be transformed by the renewing of your mind. Then you will be able to test and approve what God's will is—his good, pleasing and perfect will" (Romans 12:2).

Radical Christianity will not seek to curry the favor of the secular humanists and the left wing of the church by playing down the doctrine of the fallen nature of all mankind and the need for conversion. Rather, it will proclaim the "bad news" as unflinchingly as it joyously proclaims the "good news" of God's redemptive love in Christ Jesus. For the "good news" is robbed of its power and majesty and is infinitely devalued and cheapened when proclaimed apart from the enormity of the Fall.

Some years after the death of John, one of John's disciples, Polycarp, would write the following words to the Christians at Philippi:

These things brethren, I write to you concerning righteousness, not because I take anything upon myself, but because ye have invited me to do so. For neither I, nor any other such one, can come up to the wisdom of the blessed and glorified Paul. He, when among you, accurately and steadfastly taught the word of truth in the presence of those who were then alive. And when absent from you, he wrote you a letter, which, if you carefully study, you will find to be the means of building you up in that faith which has been given you, and which, being followed by hope, and preceded by love towards God, and Christ, and our neighbor, *is the mother of us all* (italics mine).[20]

Martin Luther would later write of Paul's letter to the church at Rome:

Therefore, it seems as if St. Paul had intended this epistle to set out, once for all, the whole of Christian doctrine in brief, and to be an introduction preparatory to the whole of the Old Testament. For there can be no doubt that if we had this epistle well and truly in our hearts, we should possess the light and power found in the Old Testament. Therefore, every Christian ought to study Romans regularly and continuously. May God grant His grace to this end. Amen.[21]

Notes

1. Enslin, *The Ethics of Paul*, Introduction, xi-xii.

2. Ernst Käseman, *Perspectives on Paul* (Philadelphia: Fortress Press, 1971), 80.

3. Ibid., 1.

4. Ibid., 24.

5. J. Gresham Machen, *The Origin of Paul's Religion* (Grand Rapids: William B. Eerdman's Publishing Company, 1925), 277-278.

6. The writings of Paul are the first "Christian" writings. Galatians was one of his early epistles.

7. C. H. Dodd, *The Meaning of Paul for Today* (Cleveland: The World Publishing Company, 1957), 53.

8. Sanders, *Paul and Palestinian Judaism*, 114-15.

9. Roland Bainton, *The Reformation of the Sixteenth Century* (Boston: Beacon Press, 1952), 69-70. Again we wish to point out that the Continental Anabaptism dealt with by Luther, Zwingli, and Calvin is not to be identified with the English Baptist movement.

10. Albert Outler, *Theology in the Wesleyan Spirit*, 33. See also letter to Charles Wesley after preaching at St. Anne's Cathedral.

11. Albert Outler, ed., *John Wesley*, (New York: Oxford University Press, 1964), 138-139.

12. Ladd, *A Theology of the New Testament*, 529-530.

13. C. H. Dodd, *The Apostolic Preaching* (Cleveland: The World Publishing Company, 1957), 8.

14. J. Murray, *Principles of Christian Conduct*, quoted in Ladd, *A Theology of the New Testament*, 528.

15. Once again we discern the influence of Continental Anabaptism on the modern Evangelical movement.

16. Ladd, *A Theology of the New Testament*, 223.

17. Clark Pinnock, quoted in *Christianity Today*, 12 December 1980, 64.

18. Francis A. Schaeffer, *The Great Evangelical Disaster* (Westchester, Ill.: Crossway Books, 1984), 119.

19. Harold Fickett, "Academia and the Church Militant," *Eternity*, December 1986, 26.

20. The Epistle of Polycarp to the Philippians.

21. Luther, Preface to Romans.